ROUTLEDGE LIBRARY EDITIONS:
ECONOMICS AND SOCIETY

Volume 20

INVESTMENT ECONOMICS

INVESTMENT ECONOMICS

J. L. CARR

Routledge
Taylor & Francis Group
LONDON AND NEW YORK

First published in 1969 by Routledge & Kegan Paul Ltd.

This edition first published in 2026
by Routledge
4 Park Square, Milton Park, Abingdon, Oxon OX14 4RN

and by Routledge
605 Third Avenue, New York, NY 10158

Routledge is an imprint of the Taylor & Francis Group, an informa business

British Library Cataloguing in Publication Data
A catalogue record for this book is available from the British Library

ISBN: 978-1-032-97576-4 (Set)
ISBN: 978-1-041-14447-2 (Volume 20) (hbk)
ISBN: 978-1-041-14449-6 (Volume 20) (pbk)
ISBN: 978-1-003-67447-4 (Volume 20) (ebk)

DOI: 10.4324/9781003674474

Publisher's Note
The publisher has gone to great lengths to ensure the quality of this reprint but points out that some imperfections in the original copies may be apparent.

Disclaimer
The publisher has made every effort to trace copyright holders and would welcome correspondence from those they have been unable to trace.

Investment Economics

by J. L. Carr

LONDON
ROUTLEDGE & KEGAN PAUL

*First published 1969
by Routledge & Kegan Paul Ltd
Broadway House, 68-74 Carter Lane
London, E.C.4
Printed in Great Britain
by Northumberland Press Limited
Gateshead*

SBN 7100 6341 5 (c)
SBN 7100 6344 x (p)

General editor's introduction

There can be no doubt that investment decision making is an important activity in almost all firms, and in many if not a majority of firms it is the major task for senior management. Although the theory of investment has a long history in economics and its central problem, the dependence of the present value of benefits and costs on their dates of occurrence, was clarified and solved a long time ago, business firms have until recently persisted in the use of crude, sub-optimal methods of investment appraisal, methods which undoubtedly lead to their earning less than maximum profits. At the same time there has been a comparative neglect of the *details* of investment theory in undergraduate courses, and economists themselves did not devote sufficient time and effort to the study of the actual problems of investment that confront business firms in practice.

The last decade dominated by the growth of computers and the use of operations research has seen a considerable change in all of this. Business firms, partly prompted by the government and led to some extent by the nationalized industries, have increasingly come to realize that their previously employed rules of thumb are not satisfactory, and can no longer be justified by a lack of ability on the part of management to use more sophisticated methods. The result of this upsurge of interest has been the greater use of the techniques themselves. At the same time many problems ignored or neglected in the past have demanded to be solved, and, indeed, have been solved by economists, operations researchers, and others. Investment theory has very much come alive again, and at the undergraduate level a much greater part of degree courses is being devoted to it.

Naturally enough, when there develops a new interest in a particular part of economics, at the same time a demand for suitable textbooks emerges. Although this demand has been met to a certain extent by the existing literature, what is available is either on a very large scale or on a very small scale. There does appear to be a need for a book covering the most important parts of the field in detail and at a suitable level of scholarship while not at the same time being so long that it would take up the whole of a year's study.

The present volume meets that need both as part of the normal undergraduate course of five to ten lectures devoted to investment, and as part of various short courses devoted to management education and training. It is particularly valuable because it does not restrict its frame of reference to private enterprise but encompasses the public sector as well.

Mr J. L. Carr, the author, is well suited to his task, being both a former academic and having spent the past few years in H.M. Treasury working on, amongst other things, problems of investment appraisal. It must be emphasized, however, that he has written and is publishing this work solely in his private capacity, the views expressed being entirely personal and in no way connected with his official position at the Treasury.

M.H.P.

Contents

1
The nature of business decisions

Business decisions can for some purposes be thought of in two groups. The first group consists of decisions about what to believe. The second, with which this book is concerned, consists of decisions about how to act on one's beliefs.

All that need be said here about the first group is that certainty is rare in business—and moreover profits other than monopoly rent would soon be competed away in a trade attended with no uncertainty—so that if profits are to be made decisions have constantly to be taken against a background of general uncertainty about the future. However the businessman must somehow form hypotheses in which he and his associates can believe, since unless his decisions are based on hypotheses in which he has some degree of confidence he is just gambling. As gambling in a well-run casino is cheaper and more likely to be profitable than gambling in business (the overheads are lower and you are competing only with other gamblers), taking decisions by sticking a pin in a piece of paper is not a rational business activity. The first group of decisions therefore amount essentially to considering all the available evidence bearing on the problem and deciding what one can reasonably expect to happen if a particular course of action is chosen.

Once working hypotheses have been formed, the techniques of investment appraisal can be used to predict the profitability of various courses of action open to the firm. Of course, in some cases sophisticated appraisal techniques will be unnecessary. Particularly in the short run, many firms operate under a number of constraints which limit their choices. A firm which has a production line in being whose capacity is being fully used to produce an established product which is expected to go on selling at a profitable price for some years ahead need not keep asking itself whether it would be more profitable to scrap the plant and re-train its labour force to make something else. Nor, if a machine breaks down, is it necessary to hold up repairs until the board has had time to consider whether it is worth spending £50 to repair a link in the production chain which might cost £50,000 to replace. For various reasons there may be a reluctance to alter prices unless costs rise to an extent that reduces profits below an acceptable level, and even then the question whether prices can be raised without affecting sales so much as to make profits even lower depends for its answer more on knowledge of the market, and guesses about probable reactions of competitors, than on appraisal techniques. Inexpensive modifications to the product may be made if market research —or hunch—suggests that beneficial effects on sales would be greater than any adverse effects on costs, and, in the opposite case, cost-saving innovations may be made without much deliberation if it seems clear that they will not have significant adverse effects on sales revenue. A firm which has no problem of excess capacity, or of inability to meet demand, and no desire to diversify, may prosper for some time taking decisions in the light of experience and common sense.

But this agreeable condition cannot last. Sooner or later the question of replacing plant must arise, when costs hitherto regarded as fixed become variable. Trading conditions may alter, and even if they do not shareholders may become restive unless profits show some tendency to increase. As profits can rarely be increased without investing capital, or re-thinking strategy, decisions going beyond the simple routine ones described above usually have to be made sometime.

The nature of investment decisions is very diverse, and the most difficult part of investment appraisal is the translation of projects into terms suitable for making quantitative estimates of their effects on profitability. A project may involve building a new factory on a green field site to make something that has never been marketed before. Its appraisal calls for estimates of the costs of building and equipping the factory, recruiting and training the necessary labour force, setting up a marketing organization (including expenditure on advertising and market research), running the plant in, and making any modifications to the product or productive process that early experience shows to be necessary or desirable, as well as the costs of materials, labour, and machine time when full-scale production begins. All this has to be estimated for various levels of output, since on the other side of the ledger some kind of estimate has to be made of sales over a number of years at different prices that might be charged. There is no point in installing an optimal-sized plant with an output of a thousand units a week if market research indicates that the likely level of sales at the lowest price that would cover production costs is more like a thousand units a month.

Replacement investment

If the product is not itself an innovation the uncertainties are less, since the manufacturer will know within limits what he can charge for a product of a given standard, and how large his output must be if his costs are to be competitive. But even the relatively simple case where the manufacturer is contemplating the replacement of machinery used in the production of an established product with what seems an assured market is unlikely to be as simple as it looks on the surface. Techniques seldom stand still, and to replace an outworn machine with an exactly similar one is the exception. As innovations in production can be either labour-saving or capital-saving there may be a choice between a replacement that is more complex, and probably more costly, than the old machine, and a newer and simpler version of the old machine that does basically the same job but costs less than an identical replacement would because it is better designed and uses fuel, for example, more economically. The former, despite its cost, may be the better buy if it can be kept reasonably fully employed, but if demand is liable to fluctuate widely, or if for some reason multi-shift working is impracticable, the cheaper and simpler replacement may be preferred. In an economy characterized by full employment and rising productivity, appraisal of a labour-saving innovation must take account of the likely rate of change of wages over a future period, since labour can be expected to grow steadily more expensive in terms of its products as productivity rises.

The timing of replacement also brings problems. Figures of costs produced by accountants can be misleading in this context, as normal accounting conventions result in the balance-sheet value of plant and other capital assets being reduced annually either in some constant proportion (reducing balance method) or by equal amounts (straight line depreciation) until they are fully amortized, after which they do not figure in costs at all. This is essentially a retrospective view of costs. It tells management what costs have been incurred in the past, but cannot be expected to provide any indication of what costs of future production are likely to be. As investment appraisal is essentially a forward-looking activity, much of the information conveyed by conventional cost accounting is irrelevant to decisions about new investment. Once a machine has been installed its past cost is irrecoverable, and the cost of continuing to use it in a productive process is the sum of the costs of the labour, fuel, materials, etc., used in conjunction with it, plus whatever disposal value it may have either as second-hand plant or scrap. This is what has to be compared with the costs of buying, installing, and operating new plant that replaces it. The occasion for replacement may arise because some old machinery has become so decrepit that the cost of keeping it working for another year exceeds the capital (interest and amortization charges) on a new machine. This is the end of its useful life to all intents and purposes. But more often plant will be replaced before this stage is reached because, unless techniques stand still, new plant is likely to bring savings in labour, fuel, or other inputs which can be added to savings in repair and maintenance costs to justify earlier renewal. Or replacement may be economic because, particularly in highly competitive industries, it can be more profitable to introduce a new and improved style of product, calling for some new machinery, than to continue with the old design until the existing plant is worn out. The economics of replacement are complex, but in practice the main question is whether replacement 'this year' would be better than postponement.

The cash flow

All these multifarious effects of a decision to modify or enlarge the productive process or the output of a firm can in principle be translated into probable effects over a number of future years on the firm's cash flow, which in turn can be seen as improving or worsening the firm's overall profitability. The central purpose of investment appraisal is first to make this translation and secondly to analyse the effects on the firm's cash flow in order to assess the effects on the firm's overall profitability.

In the case of most private investment decisions, the effects on overall profitability will be decisive, though sometimes investment which does not look financially profitable in itself may be accepted because it is thought likely to affect the firm's prestige or influence in ways that, though unquantifiable, may have important effects on its long-run profitability and growth prospects. Conversely, a firm may sometimes pass up a profitable-looking investment opportunity because it does not wish to be involved in certain activities that might cause it embarrassment or loss, possibly by affecting the goodwill of suppliers or distributors. Not all consequences of business decisions can be quantified, but some of the unquantifiable ones may be important.

In the public sector, investment appraisal may additionally take account of costs and benefits that do not enter into the expenditures or receipts of the investing body. This is legitimate because the counterparts of the shareholders, whose interests have normally to be given prominence by a private firm, are not the members of the board of the public corporation concerned, but all citizens affected, whether as consumers, employees, or taxpayers. Consequently a wider view often needs to be taken on public investments than would be taken by the directors of a private company. The special considerations affecting public investment will be discussed in the concluding chapters.

Goals

A question which this book does not attempt to answer is precisely what it is that a private firm should be trying to maximize. The term 'profitability' has been used above as though its meaning were self-evident, but unless shareholders' time preferences can be known there is no direct way of comparing a dividend paid now with a larger one postponed to a later year. In any given year more profit is clearly preferable to less profit, and if the cost of capital applicable to a particular decision can be determined it is possible, subject to the uncertainty that always surrounds future outcomes, to identify the investment that will yield a profit stream whose net present value is higher than that attributable to any alternative when discounted at a rate equal to the cost of the capital needed to finance the particular project. But, as we shall see, the cost of capital is not the same for all firms, or for all projects, or for the same project undertaken by the same firm at different times. An investment that can be financed by reducing surplus liquid assets held in the form of marketable securities, for instance, is a different proposition from one that would make a large new issue of ordinary shares necessary. There is no unique rate of discount which shareholders collectively apply to their future dividend prospects, and consequently the strategic decisions on the proportion of profits to be regarded as available for reinvestment, or the distribution of the firm's resources between uses that yield high current profits and uses that seem to have superior long-term growth prospects, will be taken by a board of directors in the light of their collective wisdom. Capital budgets are seldom unlimited, and the fact that the investment appraisal department of a firm may have come to the view that the most profitable course would be to concentrate on a number of long-term schemes at the expense of activities that are currently earning the firm's bread and butter will not cause a prudent board to lose sight of the desirability of maintaining profits in the immediate future.

It is sometimes argued that the best course to follow is that which will maximize the market value of the company's equity at the time the decision is announced. But, apart from the difficulty of judging what effect a decision to expand or contract some line of business would be likely to have on share values in the immediate future, there is no reason to believe that what the market thinks is the best course at any time will in fact be more advantageous for the shareholders in the long run than some alternative. The market is made up of a large number of more or less ill-informed people, many of whom, as Lord Keynes expressed it, 'devote their intelligences to anticipating what average opinion expects the average opinion to be'. The directors and managers of a company ought to be better informed about their own firm's prospects than 'the market', and unless we assume that the majority of shares are held by speculators looking for quick capital gains, the policies that will best serve the interests of the holders of the majority of shares will not necessarily be those which will have the most immediately favourable effects on share prices.[1]

Another idea that is occasionally canvassed is that a firm should aim to maximize the rate of return on its assets. This sounds fine, until one realizes that, literally interpreted, this would imply that a firm should sell off or wind up all its interests except the one that is currently most profitable, and return the capital to the shareholders. The same fallacy underlies the erroneous view that an investment that offers a higher rate of return on its capital cost than an alternative must be preferable to that alternative. This is not so if the incremental return on the additional capital needed for the more costly alternative is higher than its opportunity cost (see chapter 4). An investment is profitable if it adds to the amount per share available for distribution, irrespective of how it may affect the overall ratio of profits to assets in any particular case.

In the face of these difficulties we shall simply assume that the task of the investment analyst is discharged when he has indicated how profitable individual investments can be expected to be on the basis of the apparent cost of the capital required in each case, and leave on one side the intriguing question of whether it is even conceptually possible, without knowledge of shareholders' time preference functions which we cannot possess, to find criteria to determine the optimal overall strategy.[2]

NOTES

[1] Keynes: *General Theory of Employment, Interest, and Money*, 1st edition (Macmillan, 1936), p. 156.

[2] For further discussion of this question see B. Hällsten: *Investment and Financing Decisions* (Stockholm, 1966).

2
The cash flow

Business decisions that increase profitability usually lead to increased net receipts (cash inflows). An increase in net receipts may be achieved by reducing costs without similarly reducing gross receipts, by increasing gross receipts without equally increasing costs, or by affecting both receipts and costs in such a way that the excess of the former over the latter is increased. If new capital expenditure has to be incurred in order to achieve an improvement in net receipts, the improvement will be preceded by a cash outflow. To estimate the profitability of a projected investment, the first step is to compare this increased outflow with the increased inflows of cash that are expected to follow. There may also be cases in which an early inflow of cash can be secured at the cost of a subsequent deterioration in net receipts: for example, it may be possible to dispose of a valuable building or site in London for cash, transferring the activities formerly carried on there to a provincial or suburban centre where transport costs may be higher, and more managerial time may be consumed in travelling between the out-of-town centre and the London head office. Either way, the expected results can be translated into probable effects on the firm's cash flow over a number of future years.

Profitability depends not merely on the comparison between the total effects on inflows and outflows over the life of a project, but on the timing of outflows and inflows. As we shall see when we come to the chapter on discounting, receipts and expenditures falling earlier in time are more significant than those occurring later. Therefore the effects on cash flow should be presented in the form of a timetable, showing the estimated effects on outflows and inflows in each of a number of successive accounting periods (years).

Obviously what matters is the effect on the firm's overall cash flow. Occasionally an entirely new project may be financially self-contained, in the sense that it will involve outflows, and generate inflows, that do not in any way affect the firm's other activities. More typically, cash inflows and outflows will be affected in a number of different ways in future years, and some parts of the business may have to expand at the expense of others if there are constraints on the amount of finance, managerial time, or factory floorspace available. Particular care must therefore be taken not to leave out of account any foreseeable effects, favourable or unfavourable, that a decision to expand or modernize one section of a business may have on the firm's other activities.

In order to establish that a certain course of action would be advantageous it is necessary to show:

(a) that action is better than inaction, and
(b) that the course of action selected is preferable to any alternative.

It does not matter whether the decision is reached by first showing that some projected change would be profitable, and then casting around to see whether there are any more profitable alternatives, or whether we begin by showing that, if any change is to be made, a certain course is preferable to any alternative, and then asking whether the expenditure involved would be justified. The first sequence of events may in practice be more likely when a company is concerned to do something about an unprofitable area of its activities, and it is clear that some action is necessary, while the second is to be preferred if the initiative comes from an operating division which sees a way of increasing profits that are already satisfactory. In the latter case the board will expect that, before it is asked to sanction expenditure, all available alternatives will have been considered and evaluated.

In the simplest case, where the alternative to a proposed investment is to leave things as they are, the effects of the decision to invest on the firm's cash flow will be confined to the first cost of the investment, less the scrap or disposal value of any assets displaced, and the subsequent effects on costs, receipts, and tax payments as compared to what they are expected to be if the investment is not undertaken. If the proposal is to invest £100,000 on labour-saving equipment which will take a year to install and which is expected thereafter to have no effects other than to save a constant number of man-hours each year for six years, whose wage cost is estimated at £20,000 in the first year and expected to rise at 4% per year compound for the remainder of the period, the effect on cash flow would be as follows: (£ '000)

Year:	0	1	2	3	4	5	6
Cash flow:	−100	+20	+20·8	+21·6	+22·5	+23·4	+24·3

By convention, outflows or reductions in inflows are shown with minus sign, and inflows or reductions in outflows are positive. (The + sign is usually omitted as unnecessary, and in the rest of this book will not be used unless it seems occasionally necessary in the interests of clarity.) By another convention, the first or base year in a series is usually numbered 0 rather than 1. This is convenient when discounting (see next chapter), since a sum due in year 3 is discounted three years, whereas if the first year were numbered 1 it would have to be discounted for two years to bring it to its base year (year 1) value, and this could be a source of arithmetical error.

Choice between alternatives

When alternatives have to be compared, choice may be governed by the difference between the cash flows attributable to the various alternatives, rather than by the cash flows attributable to either considered as an alternative to doing nothing, because doing nothing may not be a viable alternative. For example, machinery which is an essential part of the production process of an output that is expected to remain profitable for a long time to come may have reached the end of its useful life. No one questions the need to replace this machinery, and no one is particularly interested in whether the return on its replacement would be 100%, 200%, or 500%. (These figures are quite plausible if failure to replace it would bring the whole plant to a standstill.) But there may be more and less costly ways of keeping production going, and if so there will be a choice to be made. Suppose that one possibility is to stick to the old methods, and merely replace the worn-out bits of machinery with new or re-conditioned machines, and call this course A. The alternative is to change to a new process (course B), which will be considerably more costly in terms of first cost, but which is expected to reduce future production costs and turn out a more consistent quality of product. When these respective effects on cash flow have been worked out as well as they can be estimated, the cash flows attributable to A and B respectively considered as alternatives to doing nothing can be subtracted from each other to enable the larger inflows attributable to scheme B to be compared with its additional first cost:

Year:	0	1	2	3	4	5	(£'000)
Scheme A	−50	400	400	400	400	400	
Scheme B	−200	300	500	500	500	500	
Differential cash flow	−150	−100	100	100	100	100	

(The poor result attributed to scheme B in year 1 takes account of costs of altering productive methods, re-training labour, etc.)

No management in its senses is going to employ accountants, economists, or statisticians to tell it whether it is worth spending £50,000 in order to prevent overall financial results from deteriorating by £400,000 a year for the next five years, and working out the rate of return on this investment considered as an alternative to letting the old machinery fall to pieces would be a waste of time. It would also be misleading in this case, since the most cursory inspection tells us that spending 50 to get returns of 400 a year over five years yields a higher percentage rate of return than spending 200 in order to improve results by 300 in the first year and 500 in four subsequent years. But this does not prove that it would be a mistake to spend 150 more in the first year, and accept a cost penalty due to teething troubles of a further 100 in the next year, in order to benefit by 100 in each of four succeeding years. Undiscounted, scheme B is clearly preferable. Whether it would actually be more profitable depends on the cost of capital, discussed in the following chapters.

Depreciation

It will have been noticed that the cash flow includes no provisions for depreciation. Such provisions are appropriations of profit, not factors determining profitability. They enable accountants to show in retrospect how a business has been faring, and how much cash can be distributed in dividends without reducing the firm's total assets. Obviously an investment that does not earn enough to provide for its replacement (or the return of the initial cost) before the end of its life is unprofitable, but in this case the sum of the minuses (outflows) will exceed the sum of the plus items (inflows) in the cash flow table before any discounting; all capital spent appears in the cash flow table, and to include outflows for depreciation as well would be double-counting. Depreciation provisions do not appear as cash outflows because there is in fact no need to make regular annual provisions for depreciation in the form of cash, even though it may be convenient to show such provisions in the accounts. Making a higher provision for depreciation early on will make an investment appear less profitable at the outset, but the balance will be restored in later years if equipment that has been written down to a very low value is still earning profits, and the true position can be seen only by considering the effects on the firm's cash flow over the useful life of the investment. What matters is how much the investment costs, and how it affects receipts and expenditures after it has been made, and this the cash flow reveals.

Taxation and investment grants

While provisions for depreciation do not appear in the cash flow table, tax savings resulting from depreciation allowances given against profits by the Inland Revenue constitute an important item. These were omitted in the simplified examples given above, but will now be discussed. If the investment attracts investment grant, or some other financial subvention, this too must be brought into the cash flow table. Tax payable by the company on profits resulting from the investment also has to be included, but it is usually more convenient to exclude tax deductible from dividend and interest payments, since this is affected by the company's financial structure and distribution policy, which may or may not be influenced by a particular investment decision. The net cash flow then shows the amounts available for distribution and/or appropriation to reserves, including depreciation and tax reserves, gross of any further tax that may arise on distributions. This latter will be reflected in the cost of the various types of capital (see chapters 6–8), which is expressed gross of income tax, withholding taxes, and capital gains tax. If a particular investment is expected to be wholly or partly financed by a new issue of loan or debenture stock, allowance should be made for the consequential saving of corporation tax (since loan interest is a charge against profits deductible before liability for corporation tax is arrived at).

If depreciation allowances were spread evenly over the useful earning life of assets, and tax on profits were paid in the same year as that in which the profits were made, it would be a simple matter to estimate post-tax rates of return (if pre-tax returns were known). Suppose an investment of 100 yields 30 a year (gross) for five years. With no tax the cash flow would be −100 +30 +30 +30 +30 +30. If 20 were allowed to be deducted from taxable profit each year for depreciation, and the balance were taxed at 40%, this would become:

−100 +26 +26 +26 +26 +26.

If the rate of tax rose to 50% the cash flow would be:

−100 +25 +25 +25 +25 +25.

But, as we shall see, this is quite misleading.

At the time of writing (1967) most investment in plant and machinery in the United Kingdom qualifies either for an investment grant of up to 25% (45% in development areas) or an initial allowance of up to 30%. These benefits give rise to cash inflows or reductions in outflows (tax payments) which generally fall one or two years after the investment is made. Profits are taxed in the financial year following that in which the firm's accounting year ends, and thus up to two years after they are actually earned. (This is why a provision for future tax is normally made each year out of the current profits.) Annual depreciation allowances may be on a regular (straight line) basis, but are more often computed on the reducing balance of assets, after deducting any investment grant or initial allowance. Thus in the above example, if the investment attracted grant at 25% and qualified for the maximum annual depreciation allowance of 25% of the reducing balance, the first year's annual allowance would be 25% of 75=18·75, on which the tax saved at 40% would be 7·5. In the next year the annual allowance would be 25% of (75−18·75)=14 (approximately), and tax saved would be 5·6. In each subsequent year the annual allowance decreases in the same way. After the asset had been disposed of at the end of its life with the firm a balancing allowance could be claimed, equal to any of the original cost less grant remaining undepreciated, less scrap or disposal value. (If the latter exceeded the written down value a balancing charge would be raised.) No tax would be paid on profits earned until year 2 at the earliest; in year 1 there will be a tax credit (which can be carried forward if the investing undertaking has not enough other income taxable in year 1 to take advantage of it), because the capital expenditure in year 0 can be set against other profits earned in year 0, on which tax is paid in year 1. On this basis the cash flow could be set out as follows:

Example 1

	(1)	(2)	(3)	(4)	(5)	(6)
Year	Expenditures (−) and receipts	Tax @ 40% on receipts of previous year	Investment grant	Annual allowance	Tax credit @ 40% of (4)	Net cash flow (1 − 2 + 3 + 5)
0	−100	—	—	—	—	−100
1	30		25	(19)	7·6	62·6
2	30	−12	—	(14)	5·6	23·6
3	30	−12	—	(10)	4·0	22·0
4	30	−12	—	(8)	3·2	21·2
5	30	−12	—	(6)	2·4	20·4
6	—	−12	—	(18)	7·2	−4·8

In the above simplified example it is assumed that profits start to flow in the year after that in which the capital is spent, and that the equipment has no value when it reaches the end of its life, so that a balancing allowance equal to the written down value of the original cost less grant can be claimed in year 6. (This might happen if the scrap value just covered the costs of dismantling the equipment, so that a scrap merchant was willing to remove it without making any charge or payment.) The annual depreciation allowances are shown in brackets because, like the firm's provisions for depreciation—which may or may not be the same as the Inland Revenue allowances—they do not form part of the cash flow, and appear above merely to substantiate the tax credits shown in the next column. It is assumed that the firm has enough taxable profits from its other activities in year 1 to claim the benefit of the annual allowance given in respect of capital spent in year 0. The investment grant, also received in year 1, is regarded as a capital receipt and is not taxable. If the investment did not qualify, or did not all qualify, for an investment grant, the grant (or part of it) would in most cases be replaced in year 1 by an additional tax credit equal to 40% of an initial allowance up to 30% of the original cost, and the first year's annual allowance would be calculated on the cost less initial allowance instead of on the cost less investment grant.

The series −100, +62·6, +23·6, +22·0, +21·2, +20·4, −4·8 is obviously very different from −100, +26, +26, +26, +26, +26. The rate of return, as we shall see, is also very different, and bears little relation to that implicit in the pre-tax cash flow of −100, +30, +30, +30, +30, +30. It is in fact almost impossible to guess accurately at the rate of return implied by a fluctuating cash flow, since averaging is misleading unless the flows fluctuate regularly about a mid-point. In order to find what the return is we have to use discounting, which is described in the next chapter.

When an investment is self-contained, in the sense that it is expected to cease to have any effect on the firm's cash flow after a certain date, the cash flow attributable to it is in principle a simple concept, though there may be great uncertainties in practice. Difficulties may arise where projects are not expected to come to an end tidily at some future time; this may be because some assets last longer than others, or because adoption of a project involves changes in working methods or organization that will not necessarily be reversible at the end of the lives of the major assets. When this happens it is usual to take an arbitrary time horizon, if possible approximating to the expected earning lives of the major assets. If this extends over more than about ten years, the cash flow up to the time horizon can in most cases be used as the basis for calculating prospective profitability, since this is unlikely to be much affected by minor adjustments on either side of the account for relatively distant years. If the time horizon is closer, it may make for greater accuracy if account is taken of prospective residual earning power of assets not life-expired, and of any other credits or debits that may remain as a consequence of the investment decision. These items can be capitalized and brought into the final year's cash flow at their value in that year. To do this it is necessary to use an appropriate rate of interest and employ discounting techniques.

3
Discounting: present value

The cash flow itself tells us nothing about the profitability of an investment. The mere fact that total expected receipts exceed total expected costs is not an indication of profitability unless the rate of interest is zero. Even investments which promise receipts substantially greater than their costs will not always be profitable—it depends on how long you have to wait for the receipts. If you invested £100 today, and received back £200 after twenty years, you would have done better to deposit your £100 in a building society at 4% interest, which would have given you £219 after twenty years' accumulation. By the same token, if you financed the investment by borrowing the £100 at 4% annual interest, you would go bankrupt.

If the rate of interest is greater than zero a sum of money available now is worth more than the same sum accruing at some future date. Similarly, £100 spent now costs more than the same sum to be spent in future. How much more depends on the length of time elapsing and the rate of interest, or discount rate. If this is 5%, £100 spent or received in year 0 is equivalent to £105 in year 1 or to £95·24 in year −1. £100 is thus the present value in year 0 of either £105 in year 1 or £95·24 in year −1. It is also equivalent to £163 in year 10, £265 in year 20, and £339 in year 25. (We assume for simplicity that all sums are due at the same date in each year, or else that they are spread evenly through the year.) The present value at 5% discount of £100 due in year 1 is £95·24 in year 0; if the £100 were due in year 10 its year 0 value would be £61·4, while if it were not due until year 50 it would be worth only £8·72 in year 0. More generally, the present value of any sum P due to be received or spent in n years time $= \frac{P}{(1+r)}$ where r is the rate of discount.

There are two ways of calculating the profitability of an investment from its estimated effect on cash flow. The first and simplest can be used only when a discount rate has been specified. In principle the discount rate should be equal to the estimated cost of capital to the investing undertaking, a subject which will be discussed in the next section of this book. This is the minimum rate of return which a firm has to aim to earn on its new investments if it is to expand, since if it earns less it will find difficulty in attracting new capital for expansion, while its ability to finance investment from internal resources (depreciation provisions and undistributed profits) will obviously be limited if profits are low. As directors hold office only while they retain the confidence of shareholders, any notion that growth can be sustained for long by deciding to give up paying dividends so that all the profits can be reinvested can be dismissed.

The cost of capital is discussed in chapters 6 to 8. In this chapter it will be assumed, for illustrative purposes, that the firm regards a return of 10% after corporation tax as the minimum needed to justify new investment. If this looks rather high relative to the rates of 4% and 5% mentioned above, the following considerations should be borne in mind:

(i) The 4¼% paid in 1967-8 by most large building societies on share accounts is free of income tax, but income tax has to be deducted from dividends paid out of profits that have already borne corporation tax, and capital appreciation associated with ploughing back of profits eventually attracts gains tax.

(ii) All commercial investment is risky, and a prudently

managed firm aims to build up reserves against possible future difficulties.

(iii) New capital issues are expensive, and market conditions not always favourable. Consequently firms which are expanding normally aim to finance a proportion of their new investment from retained profits.

The assumption that 10% is the minimum return required on investment carries the implication that the firm prefers £100 accruing at the end of 1968 to £109 accruing at the end of 1969, and would rather spend £109 in 1969 than £100 in 1968. It is indifferent between £100 in 1968, £110 in 1969, £121 in 1970 . . . . or £314 in 1980. Therefore an investment is profitable enough to be attractive only if the present value of all expected receipts discounted to a base year at 10% per annum exceeds the similarly discounted value in the same year of all capital and current costs. Thus the net cash flow attributable to the investment must have a positive value when all items are discounted to the base year at 10% per annum. If the cash flow sums to zero when discounted at 10%, the return on the investment must be exactly 10%, which makes it a marginal investment.

We now see how the project whose cash flow was discussed in the previous chapter would appear to a firm seeking a minimum return of 10%. Column (1), below, sets out the net cash flow as in column (6) of example 1 in chapter 2. Column (2) gives the discount factor for each equivalent to an interest charge of 10% per year. Column (3) shows the present (year 0) value of all outgoings discounted at 10%, and column (4) the present value of receipts. Subtracting the total of column (3) from that of column (4) gives the net present value of the investment at 10% discount, which may be thought of as an expression of the capitalized value of the profits expected over and above the basic 10%. For the sake of realism we assume that the units are £'000s.

Example 2

Year	(1) Net cash flow	(2) 10% discount factor	(3) Present value in year 0 (Payments)	(4) (Receipts)	(£'000)
0	−100	1·000	−100		
1	+ 62·6	0·909		56·9	
2	23·6	0·826		19·5	
3	22·0	0·751		16·5	
4	21·0	0·683		14·5	
5	20·4	0·621		12·7	
6	− 4·8	0·564	− 2·7		
			−102·7	120·1	(122·8−100 =22·8)

The net cash flow attributable to this investment has a positive present value of £17,400 in year 0. In relation to the first cost of £100,000 this prospect of profit has to be judged against the risks involved. The treatment of risk is discussed in chapter 5, but it is worth noting in passing that, since virtually all investment is attended with some uncertainty—as distinct from risks that can be calculated actuarially—no numerical criterion can be regarded as giving a clear-cut indication that a project should or should not go forward. All that can be deduced from the fact that net present value is positive is that, if expectations are fulfilled, the investment will yield more than 10%. Investment appraisal techniques do not replace managerial judgment so much as assist it by showing how profitable a given project will be if expectations are realized, enabling investments to be compared and evaluated in a less haphazard way than is possible if more rough and ready criteria—some of which may be positively misleading—are employed. It is not the purpose of this book to explain the variety of more or less inaccurate criteria that have at times been favoured by industrialists, but it is worth noting that all methods which average profits over a number of years suffer from the drawback that they neglect the all-important matter of when payments are made and received. Since true profit must be calculated with reference to the amount of capital invested and the time during which it is invested, no appraisal technique which neglects timing can be relied on. Consider the following simplified example. Project A is connected with production of something that will have a high novelty value for about two years, after which profits will fall drastically. B is a so-called growth project which will only realize its full potential towards the end of its four-year life. Both projects are expected to earn the same total amount (£120,000) over four years, and both have the same first cost (£100,000). If the £20,000 profit is averaged over the four-year life in each case, either project could be represented as earning 5% per year on its first cost or (to make it look a bit better) 10% on a notional figure of half the first cost deemed to be the average capital employed. But if these two projects are appraised correctly

Example 3

A

Year	Net cash flow	Discount factor 10%	Present value (o) −	+
0	−100	1·000	100	
1	50	0·909		45·45
2	40	0·826		33·04
3	20	0·751		15·02
4	10	0·683		6·83
			−100+100·34=+0·34	

B

Year	Net cash flow	Discount factor 10%	Present value −	+ (£'000)
0	−100	1·000	100	
1	10	0·909		9·09
2	20	0·826		16·52
3	40	0·751		30·04
4	50	0·683		34·15
			−100+89·80=−10·20	

by discounting their cash flows, A is seen to be just profitable assuming there is no risk if the cost of capital is 10%, whereas B would produce a loss. B would also be less attractive in a risk situation, since a firm investing in A gets half its money back after one year, and 90% after two years, whereas if B is chosen only 30% of the capital is returned in the first two years.

Another rough-and-ready criterion sometimes employed is the pay-out period. An investment which recoups its first cost sooner than another is judged to be better than the other. This method certainly cannot be charged with neglecting time, and if used to appraise A and B (above) it would correctly show A as more profitable than B, as the cost of A is recovered in 3 years as against 4 years for B. But if B showed returns of 20, 40, and 50 in years 1, 2, and 3 respectively it would have the same pay-out period as A, though the latter would still be the better investment. More seriously, the pay-out method neglects returns accruing after the first cost is recovered; if B above went on producing rising earnings for a further year, yielding a profit of 60 in year 5, it would become more profitable than A, since 60 discounted for 5 years at 10% has present value 37·26, raising the present value of receipts from 89·8 to 127·06 and making the net present value of the investment +27·06 as against +0·34 for A.

There is no point in arguing about whether pay-out is more or less unreliable than average return on capital employed, because there is no sense in using a potentially misleading criterion when perfectly good and simple methods of appraisal are available. Reliance on inaccurate or misleading methods causes firms to miss profitable investment opportunities and/or to engage in unprofitable ventures. In the long run this must reduce profit unless we make the implausible assumption that errors in appraisal always cancel out errors in forecasting costs or receipts. This is about as realistic as assuming that fine weather will always occur at week-ends.

4

Rate of return

Although the profitability of an investment is simply and unambiguously expressed by its net present value at a stated discount rate, it is often useful to know the rate of return on capital invested. The cost of capital may be uncertain, for example, particularly if one is looking a long way ahead. Some people concerned with taking decisions, or providing finance, especially at a senior level, may be more accustomed to thinking in terms of rate of return than in terms of present value. For reasons that will appear below, investment decisions should preferably not be taken on the basis of rate of return alone—except where it is obvious that a project is either so unprofitable, or so much more profitable than any alternative, that there is no problem. But it may often be useful to know the rate of return as well as the present value.

The rate of return in the sense in which the term is used in this chapter is not the ratio of average annual book profits to the cost of an investment, or to the average capital employed. The true rate of return on the capital invested, variously called the internal rate of return, d.c.f. (discounted cash flow) rate of return, or break-even rate of return, takes account of the time during which capital remains invested as well as its amount. To calculate it we start with the cash flow, and find by trial and error the rate of discount that equates the present value of all receipts to the present value of all costs in a base year, so that net present value sums to zero. (The rate of return can also be computed mathematically or approximated by interpolation. We remarked in the previous chapter that, if the net present value of an investment was 0 when the cash flow was discounted at 10%, the rate of return would be 10%. This is because, if there is no surplus and no deficit left over when all costs and receipts are brought back to a base year at 10%, the receipts must be just sufficient to repay the initial cost over the life assumed, after paying interest at 10% on the balance outstanding each year. The easiest way to grasp the significance of the internal rate of return is to imagine that an investment being appraised is to be financed entirely out of a bank overdraft used exclusively for the project. When operations begin, the account is overdrawn to the amount of all expenditure incurred during the construction and running-in period (if any), plus accrued interest. During the earning life all receipts are paid into the single account and go to reduce the overdraft, while all expenses come out of the account. At the close of operations, the account is credited with the disposal value of any assets left over. If the same rate of interest is charged throughout, there will be a surplus left in the account if the internal rate of return over the whole period exceeds the rate of interest charged, and a deficit if the rate of interest exceeds the rate of return. If the two are equal the investment will break even, hence the term 'break-even rate of return'.

The principle can be illustrated by referring back to project A in example 3 in the previous chapter, which had a net present value almost equal to zero (+0·34) when discounted at 10%, indicating that the rate of return was just over 10%. Assuming for the sake of simplicity that all payments and receipts fall at the end of each year, the imaginary overdraft bearing interest at 10% would vary as in example 4 on the next page.

If the residual balance of +0·54 outstanding at the end of year 4 is discounted back five years to the start of year 0 at 10% (i.e. multiplied by 0·621), it is seen to be equal to the net present value of +0·34. Of course, in practice receipts and payments do not fall neatly at the beginning

Example 4

Year	Balance O/S 1 Jan.	Interest @ 10% for year	Cash flow during year	Balance O/S 31 Dec.	(£'000)
0	—	—	−100	−100	
1	−100	−10	+ 50	− 60	
2	− 60	− 6	+ 40	− 26	
3	− 26	− 2·6	+ 20	− 8·6	
4	− 8·6	− 0·86	+ 10	+ 0·54	

or end of years, and the process of calculating the exact rate of return is less simple than in the above artificially simplified example, but the principle is not affected.

To see how we find the rate of return on an investment which does not conveniently have a present value close to zero when discounted at the selected rate we can look at project B in example 3. This had a negative present value of −10·2 at 10%, indicating a return less than 10%. We try a lower discount rate (5%) at which the investment has appreciable positive present value (see below). Interpolating, we find that at 6% it almost breaks even. Since it is obvious that 6% is closer to the break-even rate

Example 5

Year	Net cash flow	Discount factor 5%	Present value @ 5%	Discount factor 6%	Present value @ 6%
0	−100	1·000	−100	1·000	−100
1	+ 10	0·952	9·52	0·943	9·43
2	+ 20	0·907	18·14	0·890	17·80
3	+ 40	0·864	34·56	0·840	33·60
4	+ 50	0·823	41·15	0·792	39·60
			−100		−100
			+103·37		+100·43

than 7% (or even 6½%) we describe the rate of return as 6%. There is normally little point in greater precision, since in investment appraisal we are necessarily dealing with figures derived from forecasts of future sales, prices, and production costs, and the 'best guess' on which calculations are necessarily based is always subject to some margin of error. But the rate of return can of course be calculated precisely if necessary.

Where only a simple accept-or-reject criterion is required, and the case is a simple one involving an initial cash outflow, or series of outflows, followed by a stream of cash inflows, to show that a project offers a rate of return higher than whatever minimum is deemed necessary to justify acceptance is enough. (It amounts to the same thing as showing that it has positive net present value when the cash flow is discounted at a rate equal to the minimum return desired.)

Comparisons and difficulties

But in more complex cases some further steps are required before rate of return can be a satisfactory criterion. If choice has to be made between investments that are alternatives, it will not always be the one with the highest rate of return that is the best use of the firm's resources. If capital costs are the same, rate of return will usually be a reliable guide, but if costs differ it is necessary to look at the return on the incremental cost of the larger of two investments in order to see whether the additional capital expenditure is justified. (The incremental return has to be compared with the cost of the increment of capital needed, which may be higher than the cost of the capital required for the cheaper alternative—see chapters 6 to 10.) A more costly investment offering a higher rate of return than a cheaper alternative may be unattractive in high-risk situations, or if the extra cost would make a new share issue necessary. On the other hand, a large investment offering a return that exceeds the marginal cost of capital to the firm may be more profitable than a cheaper alternative offering a higher rate of return. This can happen if the total profit flowing from the more costly investment is expected to be greater, and the difference in profit represents an adequate return on the extra capital required. To take an extremely simple example, an investment of 200 that yields 25 a year for ever (12½%) could be preferred to an alternative costing 100 and yielding 13 a year for ever (13%) if the cost of capital was less than 12%. This is because investing the second 100 increases profits by 12 a year (25−13), and by assumption this is better than any alternative employment of the second 100 if the marginal cost of capital is less than 12%.

Calculating the return on an incremental cash flow is not always straightforward. So far we have considered flows in which an initial outflow or series of outflows is followed by a stream of inflows. When cash flows of this type are discounted, raising the discount rate always reduces present value because the inflows, being more distant in time, are discounted proportionately more heavily than the preceding outflows. If the undiscounted inflows exceed the undiscounted outflows there will always be one (and only one) positive discount rate at which the present value of the inflows will equal that of the outflows, which expresses the rate of return per unit of capital outstanding per unit of time accurately and unambiguously. Equally, of course, a cash flow that consists of an initial inflow or series of inflows followed by a stream of outflows can be evaluated by finding the discount rate that makes the present values of total inflows and outflows equal. This is not exactly a return on capital invested, since initially there is disinvestment rather than investment. But a firm which has the opportunity of securing a benefit (cash inflow) in the immediate future at the cost of a subsequent deterioration in its cash flow will want to know whether the short-term advantage is worth the longer run cost. If the undiscounted inflow is greater than the (subsequent) undiscounted outflows there is no problem, since 100 received now is always preferable to 99 (or 100) to be paid later. (If you were told that the cash price of a car was £500 but that you could have it now on payment of the first part of twelve monthly instalments of £40, you should not need a formal training in economics to tell you which course to choose.) But if the sum of the undiscounted outflows exceeds that of the undiscounted inflows, a rational decision can only be made by ascertaining whether the discount rate that equates the two is higher or lower than the cost of capital. In this case, of course, the break-even rate must be lower than the cost of capital to make the proposition acceptable, since in a cash flow of this type raising the discount rate reduces the present value of the outflows relative to that of the inflows that precede them, and so increases the present value of the stream.

A cash flow that is made up of an alternating or irregular series of inflows and outflows is less easy to appraise. It may be possible to find a single discount rate that reduces its net present value to zero, but this cannot always be taken as a proper measure of the earning power of the project to which the cash flow attaches. Whether it can be so regarded or not depends on whether there are any periods of negative investment.

We have seen that the internal rate of return measures the return per unit of capital invested per unit of time. To revert to our analogy of the bank overdraft, this is the highest rate the borrower could afford to pay on the outstanding balance of the overdraft during the period of the investment if he were to end up all square at the end. If the rate of return is 20%, the investor will make a profit if the rate charged on the outstanding balance is less than 20%, assuming that he remains overdrawn to some extent throughout the period. But if at some stage his account is in credit, as it may be even if the break-even rate of 20% is charged if there are cash outflows towards the end of the period for which provision is made out of profits earned earlier, the calculation that tells us that 20% is the rate of return will have implicitly assumed that this is the rate of interest earned on credit balances arising during the term of the investment, as well as the rate paid on debit balances. In marginal investments where the rate of return is equal or nearly equal to the cost of capital this assumption may be correct, provided that temporary cash surpluses can in fact be invested to earn returns similar to the cost of capital for the main investment, but the assumption obviously will flatter investments yielding more than the cost of capital (by crediting them with interest on temporary credit balances exceeding that which will in fact be received), and conversely makes unprofitable investments look even worse than they really are.

Multiple solutions

As well as being misleading, the internal rate of return on an irregular cash flow may not be unique. As we have seen, raising the discount rate always reduces the present value of a stream in which all the outflows precede all the inflows, and increases the present value of a stream in which the inflows precede the outflows. But if outflows and inflows alternate, raising the discount rate may increase the present value, reduce it, or leave it unchanged. The last result happens if the effect of a higher discount rate in reducing the value of future inflows is exactly offset by its effect in increasing the present value of future outflows (recalling that a reduction in a minus item is equivalent to an increase in a plus item).

An irregular cash flow can be adjusted so that a unique and meaningful rate of return can be found. This is often simple enough. When the last item in a cash flow is negative—perhaps because tax on the profits earned in the last year of an asset's life *is* not paid until the following year—a small final outflow can be discounted back to the last earning year at a rate equal to the rate of interest a cash provision for future tax payments might be expected to earn during the year before payment becomes due, or something higher if temporary cash surpluses can be more productively employed in the firm's business. The negative flows at the end being eliminated, the last inflow is reduced by the discounted value of the outflow(s) that have disappeared. Thus:

−800 +200 +300 +400 +200 −100 becomes
−800 +200 +300 +400 +109·1

if the cost of capital is 10%,

or −800 +200 +300 +400 +104·8

if the cost of capital is 5%. This technique for eliminating stray outflows can in principle be used to reduce any cash flow stream to a form in which a unique and meaningful internal rate of return can be found, but calculation sometimes gets rather complex, and then it may be easier to find the present value of the whole series discounted at a rate equal to the cost of capital, and use this as a criterion. This is quite satisfactory if one and the same cost of capital expresses both the rate which temporary cash surpluses can be expected to earn and the return acceptable on the whole project. Where this is not so, or where the cost of capital is not uniform throughout the investment period, a financing plan will be needed—see chapter 8. For a fuller discussion of the problems of calculating rates of return when cash flows are irregular, see 'The Financial Attractiveness of a Project', by A. M. Duguid and J. G. Laski, in *Operational Research Quarterly*, vol. 15, no. 4, pp. 317-28.

5
Risk and uncertainty

So far we have assumed that the cash flows to be analysed express the probable consequences of a decision to invest, without asking how probable these consequences are or by how much out-turns may diverge from expectations. This is obviously unrealistic. All forecasts of future events are uncertain, and some investments will obviously appear more risky than others. At one extreme, for example, a project may involve merely replacing a relatively inexpensive piece of equipment that is an essential component in a production line manufacturing an established product that seems unlikely to go out of fashion or be superseded in the foreseeable future. This is almost riskless, since the cost is likely to be recovered very quickly if the consequence of failure to replace the machine would be to bring the production line to a standstill and forfeit an annual profit that may be several times the cost of replacing the outworn component. At the opposite extreme one might consider a large investment in a politically unstable foreign country necessary to develop an invention that has not yet been tested in production, let alone marketed successfully, and which will be profitable only if a world-wide market can be developed and exploited before the product is made obsolete by a technically more advanced one on which a large American firm is known to be working.

Coming back to earth for a moment, we can register the fact that the basic uncertainty that attaches to all future returns is expressed adequately by the use of a discount rate derived from the market price of risk capital, which will normally be higher than the pure rate of interest on secured loans. (If prices are unstable holders of even the best securities will be exposed to loss through inflation, and the phenomenon known as the reverse yield gap may appear. This makes the cost of risk capital, as measured by the ratio of equity dividends to share prices, look lower than the rate of interest on government bonds. But of course investors buy low-yielding equities only in the expectation that dividends and capital values will at least keep pace with prices, and the true cost of risk capital is not the ratio of dividends to share prices but the discount rate that equates the present value of the stream of future dividends that shareholders expect to the price of the share. If investors are rational this must be appreciably higher than the current rate of interest on secured loan stocks, since an irregular and uncertain stream of future dividends will always appear less desirable than a steady stream of guaranteed interest payments with the same present value.)

The cost of capital will be discussed in the following chapters. For the time being it is enough to note that general uncertainty about the future is taken into account by the use of a discount rate derived from the price of risk capital rather than riskless loans to discount future returns. Additional risks that are closely related to the time that must elapse between investment outlays and the accrual of profits can be taken into account by using a still higher discount rate than the general rate derived from the market price of risk capital. Alternatively, a time horizon can be used to leave out of account returns that are hoped for, rather than expected, in the more distant future.

These methods are arbitrary and unsatisfactory, however, where risks are not specifically related to time. In the case of a new and untried product, for example, the main risk may be that the venture will never get off the ground. If it once becomes established, and teething troubles are overcome, it may be possible to look forward to continuing profits with a fair degree of confidence. In this kind of venture it would obviously be wrong to regard the prospective returns in the early years as relatively riskless, and discount the later years more heavily.

Two kinds of risk that deserve to be distinguished are:

(i) the risk implicit in a wider range of possible outcomes—an investment that may yield anything from −20% to +40% is more risky than one expected to yield something between +5% and +15%;

(ii) the risk of a greater probability of an unfavourable outcome—an investment that will be profitable only if three out of the next four August Bank Holidays are fine is more risky than an investment that is unaffected by the weather, and one where the whole of the capital invested will be lost if anything goes wrong is more risky than one in which something can be salvaged from the wreck unless everything goes wrong.

In either case it is desirable to draw up a table showing various possible outcomes before attempting to reach a decision. However, it will seldom be helpful to present management with an unqualified statement to the effect that the rate of return on a proposed investment might lie anywhere between −20% and +40%, or that the result might be anything from a loss of £50,000 to a profit of £150,000. In some cases it may be possible to assign numerical probabilities to each of a number of possible outcomes, and if this is so the range of possibilities can be epitomized by a single figure, provided that the firm's risk aversion function is known. This last is an important qualification, since few firms are so financially strong that the risk of losing £1 million can be accepted with the same equanimity as the loss of £1000. But where meaningful numerical probabilities can be assigned to outcomes, the mathematically probable result, derived from a weighted average of all possible outcomes, plus a supporting statement drawing attention to the magnitude of possible losses and the length of time for which the major portion of the capital will be at risk, should be enough to enable management to make up its mind whether to proceed.

Uncertainty

Unfortunately it is seldom possible to find objective criteria for calculating mathematical probabilities outside the area of what are known as insurable risks. If probabilities cannot be calculated, the investment analyst cannot be expected to provide management with an assessment that points clearly to a decision one way or the other, unless the risks of loss turn out on examination to be either so small or so improbable that they can be neglected, or so large in relation to likely gains that no one in his senses would risk either his own or the shareholders' money on the project. In the grey area between investments that are obviously worth while and those which are equally obviously not on, appraisal techniques can still help the decision-making process by setting out clearly the conditions in which various levels of profit or loss can be expected, evaluating the consequences of the various unknown factors that can be expected to affect the outcome, and drawing management's attention to the key variables. Surrounding any major investment decision there will be a number of uncertainties, which will affect the outcome in greater or lesser degree. By calculating the effect on present value or rate of return of making different assumptions about the main variables, it is possible to isolate those which are critical. Estimates can then be made of the profits or losses that would be made if any (or all) of these key variables diverged significantly from its assumed value, and armed with this information the entrepreneur is better placed to make a rational judgment than he would be if he had to form a view on the basis of a single 'most probable' outcome or, at the other extreme, a pair of figures indicating respectively how much might be gained if everything went right, and how much could be lost if everything went wrong. A good deal of confusion and pointless argument could be avoided if both businessmen and economists appreciated that the investment analyst's function is to indicate what might go wrong, and what the consequences for profitability would be if it did. To decide what risks to take and when to cut your losses is essentially part of the entrepreneurial function. Similarly it is for the entrepreneur, not his investment analyst, to decide what the firm's risk aversion function should be, in cases where the numerical probability of a certain outcome with a given range of uncertainty can be determined.

6
The cost of capital I

So far we have assumed that a supply of finance is always on tap at a fixed price, and that this price can be taken as a datum by the investment analyst. This assumption much simplified the preliminary exposition of appraisal techniques, but it needs to be critically examined before the ranking of investments in an order of preference, and choice between mutually exclusive alternatives, can be usefully discussed. Obviously, if we can assume an unlimited supply of capital at a known fixed price these problems are simple, since an investment with higher risk-adjusted present value than another when both are discounted at the unique cost of capital rate will always be a better use of resources. As the assumption of a perfectly elastic supply of capital implies that all projects with positive present value at the fixed discount rate can—and presumably will—be financed and carried out, however, the need for a ranking criterion is not obvious.

Loan capital

In the real world firms are seldom faced with horizontal supply schedules of investible funds. Loan capital will usually be cheaper than equity capital both because less risk is borne by the lender and because interest is deducted from gross profit to arrive at the taxable profit. To service 8% debentures a firm need only earn 8% after depreciation but before tax. But since risk not borne by lenders is necessarily borne by the proprietors or shareholders, there is obviously an upper limit to the proportion of its total capital which a firm will be willing to raise in the form of loans. (Even if the shareholders were willing to take bigger risks, doubts about the firm's ability to pay interest punctually and regularly on a very large amount of loan capital would result in a rise in the rate of interest at which further loans could be raised in the market.)

Retained earnings

For the majority of British companies, retained earnings are the most important source of finance for new investment. (Retained earnings of course include depreciation reserves, though provisions for depreciation are not shown as undistributed profits in companies' accounts.) The cost of using these internal funds to invest in fixed assets or stocks is an opportunity cost, since if they are not reinvested internally they can be invested outside the firm. The cost of using them internally cannot therefore be less than the expected returns from the most profitable employment that can be found for them outside the firm. (It may be higher than this if shareholders would prefer higher dividends—which they could of course invest themselves through the market after paying income tax—to the highest return obtainable on outside employments of company funds, or if the business of the company in question is so risky that a prospective return of x per cent on a diversified portfolio is more attractive than the same prospective return on internal investments.)

There are many different ways in which retained earnings may profitably be employed, apart from their use to improve or enlarge the productive capacity of the business that earned them. Diversification into other fields is one possibility; this may sometimes take the form of direct investment in new plant, buildings, etc., to be managed by the existing management, but it may seem more attractive to acquire an interest, possibly amounting to control, in a firm already established in the field. Or, if it does not wish to risk engaging in unfamiliar activities, the firm may consider taking over a competitor; even if anti-monopoly legislation prevents direct exploitation of the lesser degree of competition that will prevail after a merger, rationalization of production and marketing arrangements may be advantageous. A third possibility is to integrate vertically, by acquiring control of component suppliers or of distributors of the firm's products.

In the absence of any attractive openings of these kinds, the firm may consider acquiring shareholdings in other firms that need new capital and are expected to be profitable. Fast-growing firms typically need more capital to finance expansion than they can provide from internal sources, and a placing with a single large investor is likely to be less costly than a new market issue. As rapid growth is frequently associated with above-normal profitability, an outside investment of this kind may be attractive to a profitable but slow-growing firm with surplus liquid funds to invest. In the last resort the firm can add to its portfolio of marketable securities. Individual shareholders could of course do the same with their dividends if they wished, but as distributed profits in Great Britain are taxed more heavily than undistributed a tax advantage is gained if the company invests surplus funds directly instead of paying out higher dividends.

New share issues

The expected return on equities bought in the open market, which sets a minimum to the opportunity cost of retained earnings, is also directly relevant to the cost of new share issues. Other things equal, a new issue will appeal to investors only if it offers prospective returns as good as those expected on other shares. As some degree of market imperfection is to be expected, a new issue is unlikely to be floated successfully unless the issue price is low enough to make the new shares appear slightly more attractive than other shares currently available; this imperfection, together with the direct costs of the issue, will make new share issues generally a more costly source of finance than retained earnings.

From the point of view of existing shareholders, the extra cost imposed by market imperfection manifests itself in a fall—which may be only temporary—in the market price of the shares at the time of the new issue. Apart from the obvious losses incurred by shareholders who sell shares during the time when prices are depressed (which may date from the announcement of the issue if it leads investors to expect a fall), shareholders who do not sell any shares will suffer some loss if shares are taken up by outsiders at depressed prices, unless the new investment which the issue is to finance yields a return higher than the previous earnings yield. This is because new shareholders will have come in on a higher prospective yield basis if shares were temporarily under-valued at the time of the issue. If the overall returns to shareholders as a body are the same in the future as in the past the return to the new shareholders' equity will be more than, and the return to the old shareholders' equity less than, this overall return.

This point is best illustrated by a numerical example. Suppose the 'normal' (i.e. pre-issue) earnings yield was 10%, and the undervaluation resulting from the new issue caused this to rise temporarily to 12·5%. If 40% of the new issue was subscribed by the old shareholders and 60% by outsiders, the true cost of the new capital (ignoring issue expenses) would be approximately $(12{\cdot}5 \times 0{\cdot}6 + 10{\cdot}0 \times 0{\cdot}4) = 11{\cdot}5\%$. That is, a weighted average of the costs of the amounts subscribed by old and new shareholders. If all the issue had been taken up by new shareholders, the cost would have been 12½%.

The losses that old shareholders would suffer if this money were invested to yield only 10% can be shown by a simplified example. Suppose a company with no loan or other prior charge capital had issued in the past 100,000 £1 shares, currently valued at 40s. each, and that on this market valuation of £200,000 it was earning an annual profit of £20,000 which was expected to continue indefinitely. Now supposing it offers for sale another 100,000 shares and that the market price per share falls to 32s. (on which the old return of 4s. per share would be 12½%). The amount raised will be £160,000 and if this earns no more than 10% (on the same basis as the original £200,000) profits will increase to £36,000 and earnings per share will fall from 4s. to 3s. 7d. A shareholder who had paid 40s. for his shares in the expectation of a 10% return would be getting 9%, but a new shareholder buying at 32s. would get 11·25%. The latter would make a capital gain if the earnings ratio were later to return to 10%, since the share price would rise to 36s., but this is still below the pre-issue price of 40s.

Plainly the size and timing of a new share issue is of critical importance. The two factors (apart from issue expenses) which affect the cost are the amount taken up by outsiders and the fall in the market price needed to get these shares taken up. If either of these is zero, the other ceases to apply; if all the shares are taken and held by existing shareholders, the nominal terms of the issue will not matter to the shareholders *collectively*, since the lower the price goes, the more shares they get for their money. So long as the new assets earn a return equal to the previous earnings yield of the shares, their interests are not affected. In the other limiting case, if the market price is unaffected by the issue it does not matter what proportion is taken by outsiders, since if the earnings yield is maintained, and the share price unchanged, the old shareholders have nothing to complain about. But the likelihood that all or most of the new shares will be taken and held by existing shareholders obviously varies inversely with the size of the issue: a shareholder with £1000 of shares is more likely to be able to find £200 to take up his allocation of a 1 for 5 issue than the £500 required if the issue is 1 for 2. As the market is also likely to absorb the offered portion of a relatively small issue with less fall in price than would be needed to get a larger issue taken up (if other things are equal), it is evident that supply schedules of investible funds will generally slope upwards.

In the case instanced above the old shareholders who before the issue had assets worth £200,000 and earning £20,000 a year are presumed to have subscribed a further £64,000 in taking up 40,000 new shares at 32s. each. Assuming that the rise in earnings yield is only temporary, being due solely to imperfection of the capital market, their position will not be worse after the issue if they can lay claim to earnings of £26,400 a year, so that their shareholdings will be worth £264,000 when the earnings ratio returns to 10%. As they now own 70% of the shares, the total profit required will be 10/7ths of £26,400, or £37,700 a year. If the original assets continue to earn £20,000, the new assets in which the £160,000 proceeds of the share issue are invested must produce £17,700 a year, or rather more than 11%.

While this will suffice to protect the interests of the original shareholders collectively, individual shareholders who for one reason or another do not take up their average quota of 40 new shares for every 100 shares held will suffer losses, and any who are forced to sell shares before the earnings ratio has returned to 10% will lose still more. Partly to protect the interests of these shareholders, and partly because it is usually impossible to predict how many shares existing shareholders will take up, and where the market price will settle after a new issue, new shares are commonly offered in the first place to existing shareholders on a 'rights' basis of so many new shares for every old share held, at a price judged to be comfortably below the market price at which outsiders will take up the new shares. Thus shareholders who cannot or do not choose to invest more money in the firm can compensate themselves for the fall in the share price and in earnings per share to be expected when a new issue is made in an imperfect market by selling their 'rights' to others. It should be clear that shareholders cannot gain collectively by a low rights price, since a fall in the nominal issue price increases the number of new shares that have to be issued to raise a given sum, and so reduces the prospective market value of each share. The true cost of the issue remains determined by the amount which outside investors have to subscribe and the terms on which they are prepared to subscribe it.

7
The cost of capital II

It will be plain from the previous chapter that precise calculation of the cost of equity capital is impossible, especially when new issues are to be made. Judgment has to be exercised as to how much of the issue the market will be required to take, and the terms on which it will take it. Underwriters earn a living by making intelligent guesses as to how individual issues will go, and to the individual firm the best guide to the cost of a new share issue is probably the figure at which underwriters will agree to take up any unsold shares, plus commission and other expenses. The factors lying behind the underwriters' view are complex, and underlying them all are investors' expectations about the future.

Historical comparisons

If investors could assume that the future would resemble the past the problem would of course be much simplified. It has been suggested that the cost of equity capital can be ascertained with reasonable accuracy by looking at returns to equity investment over a long past period, preferably at constant prices and net of tax. Professor Merrett and Mr Allen Sykes have calculated returns that would have been enjoyed by hypothetical investors buying and holding ordinary shares over a succession of 11-year periods between 1919 and 1963, and the similarities between pre-war and post-war experience are sufficiently marked to suggest that there may be an underlying long-run supply price for risk capital which is little affected by changing conditions.[1] But the assumptions that have to be made if this theory is to be plausible are daunting.

The observed similarity between post-tax rates of return in the 1930s and in the 1950s implies a rise in pre-tax rates of return, since tax rates both in the U.K. and in the U.S.A. rose over the period. But the pressure of demand on capacity also rose, and in classical economic theory this rise in the pressure of demand would account for some increase in the pre-tax rate of return on capital. Those who argue that there is a constant 'underlying' price for risk capital are in effect denying that rates of return are influenced (in the long run) by the pressure of demand on capacity, and attributing the whole increase to forward shifting of corporate taxation.[2] The latter phenomenon may be explained if it is assumed that firms typically set prices by adding a mark-up margin to average total costs at some 'normal' level of output, aiming at a certain desired ratio of post-tax profits to sales. In such a situation taxes on profits form an element of cost, and full tax-shifting is the logical result. But the assumption implies a surprising absence of profit-maximizing behaviour, which one would expect to observe over a wide field of competitive industry. (Monopolists may consciously refrain from maximizing profits because to do so in their monopoly position would raise profits so far above the competitive average as to invite the emergence of competition or legislation which would in the end threaten their comfortable (and sufficiently profitable) monopoly position.)

The view that the burden of profits taxes is normally shifted forward to consumers has been extensively criticized. The statistical evidence was re-examined by R. J. Gordon in a recent article[3] which concluded that the influence of tax rates on pre-tax rates of return had been very small in U.S. manufacturing industry between 1925 and 1962. The average pre-tax return on assets rose with the rise in the average productivity of assets, but firms were not able to go beyond this in an attempt to avoid the burden of increasing corporate tax rates, or to increase their pre-tax income share relative to labour. The rise in the average productivity of capital over the period can perhaps be attributed to an increasing scarcity of capital available for investment (due to rising pressure of consumer demand and defence expenditure) together with a rapid growth in opportunities for profitable innovation created by technical progress.

It is not only tax-shifting that is in question, however. Those who argue that risk capital has a constant supply price are tacitly assuming that this price is unaffected by changes in interest rates, or by changes in the real returns to fixed interest investment caused by inflation. But on general theoretical grounds one would expect that, in a free capital market, there will be a long-run tendency for returns expected by investors in equities to be influenced by returns obtainable on fixed interest securities. And if inflation and taxation between them reduce real net returns to holders of fixed interest securities to historically low levels, it would be surprising if real net returns to equity investors remained unaffected. Such a course of events would imply that the gap between real net returns to equity and fixed interest investment would have to widen both relatively and absolutely, which is intuitively implausible. (One might in fact expect the opposite tendency, as more and more people become aware of the risk of erosion of capital invested in fixed interest securities, and of the opportunities for small investors offered by unit trusts, etc.)

The reverse yield gap

Before 1939 the greater risks inherent in equity investment caused dividend yields of equities to be somewhat higher than interest rates, but since 1959 fears of inflation and expectations of continued full employment have led to a 'reverse yield gap', and dividend yields on equities have been lower than yields of fixed interest securities. But the fact that investors' preferences as between equity and fixed interest investments can and do change over time does not alter the fact that, for most investors, the opportunity cost of an investment in an equity portfolio is the return that could have been earned by investing the same sum at fixed interest. What is certain is that, in the long run, investors will look for higher average returns, at constant prices and after tax, on equities than on relatively riskless fixed interest investments. Adam Smith in the *Wealth of Nations* suggested as a rough rule of thumb that an acceptable rate of profit might be about double the rate of interest ruling at any time. Lord Keynes a century and a half later thought that a minimum rate of interest of about 2% would be needed to overcome investors' preference for liquidity, and historically average post-tax returns on British Government securities during periods when prices were reasonably stable have probably been between 2 and 3%. If investors take the view that equities are attractive only when they offer prospective long run post-tax returns of the order of 4 to 6% at constant prices, the minimum returns required to justify employment of shareholders' capital will be of the order of 7 to 10% after corporation tax, if we take the present standard rate of income tax to typify the tax on distributions of profit. The gross returns needed to earn this cannot be calculated without knowledge of the investment grants and depreciation allowances relating to specific investment projects, and of the current tax position of the firm contemplating the investment.

Probably the most reasonable conclusion one can come to on the evidence so far available is that the real rewards necessary to overcome investors' liquidity preference and risk aversion establish a minimum long-run price for risk capital, and that the degree of tax-shifting necessary to maintain post-tax returns at or above this minimum will in the long run be achieved, because the supply of new capital coming forward would begin to dry up if the necessary minimum incentive were not provided. (This assumes that the role of the private investor is not taken over by the State.) But scarcity of capital associated with pressure of demand on resources may at times, and possibly for long periods, support returns at some higher level. During these times equity investment may be significantly more profitable than investment in fixed interest securities if capital markets are managed in such a way that interest rates are prevented from rising to the extent necessary to bring real post-tax returns to holders of fixed interest securities up to a level at which they are equal to prospective risk-adjusted post-tax returns on investment in industrial and commercial assets (the rate of profit). In the modern State, which can finance investment from taxation as an alternative to borrowing the necessary sums in the market, market rates of interest do not necessarily have to be closely related to rates of profit earned on real investment, which underlie long-term pre-tax returns to equity investors (because the profits of a company, after tax and prior charges, belong to the ordinary shareholders). But the exceptional gap between fixed interest and equity yields can be expected to continue only so long as the pressure of demand remains high enough to keep risk capital scarce in relation to opportunities for its profitable employment.

NOTES

[1] A. J. Merrett and Allen Sykes: 'Incomes Policy and Company Profitability' and 'Return on Equities and Fixed Interest Securities', *District Bank Review*, nos. 147 and 148, September–December 1963.

[2] See M. Krzyzaniak and R. Musgrave: *The Shifting of Corporation Income Tax*, Baltimore, 1963.

[3] R. J. Gordon: 'Incidence of the Corporation Income Tax in U.S. Manufacturing', *American Economic Review*, September 1967.

8

The cost of capital III: Financing plans

In some simple cases it may be possible to calculate the minimum return required to justify any prospective employment of funds by taking a weighted average of the estimated costs of the different kinds of finance—loans, internal funds (depreciation and undistributed profits) and new equity—to be employed. But this assumes that the proportions these components bear to one another are independent of whether or not a particular investment is undertaken, or of when it is undertaken. Companies that do not plan to raise any new equity capital in any circumstances may be able to use this approach provided they do not expect to see the proportion borne by loan capital to total assets alter materially. For such companies the alternative to any capital project likely to be considered will be the investment of reserve funds outside the firm, possibly in a portfolio of marketable securities, and/or some reduction in bank loans and other fixed interest liabilities. Assuming that it is prepared and able to finance a proportion of the cost of any new project by additional borrowing, or selling securities from its portfolio, where either of these courses appears more attractive than reducing dividends or neglecting other profitable opportunities for direct employment of funds, such a firm may reasonably plan to invest wherever it sees the prospect of a return exceeding the weighted average of the cost of the 'mix' of new loan capital and internal funds likely to be employed.

But this approach will be misleading if the cost of a

project is so large, in relation to internal funds available for reinvestment and unused borrowing capacity, that its acceptance means that a new issue of ordinary shares will become necessary, either immediately or at some future date earlier than the date when a new equity issue might have to be contemplated if the project under consideration were not accepted. Given that new outside equity is the most expensive form of capital, its cost can be taken to represent the marginal cost of finance in such a case, and it can easily be seen that, if the aim is to maximize profits, the marginal (least profitable) investment undertaken must show a prospective return at least equal to the marginal cost of finance. In the case of the firm that has not sufficient internal resources and unused borrowing capacity to carry out all the investments in its 'programme', rejection or postponement of any item in the programme will avoid, or at any rate postpone or reduce, a new equity issue. Since the cost of a new equity issue to the existing shareholders depends, other things equal, on the proportion sold to outsiders, which will obviously tend to increase with the amount of the issue, the size and timing of new equity issues is a factor of great importance.

Because of its greater cost, new equity finance made necessary by acceptance of a project will not necessarily be raised immediately the decision to go ahead is taken, or even in time to finance the cash outgoings associated with the project. If temporary finance is available in the form of loans or internal funds it will normally be advantageous to use this at the start and make the new issue only when it is called for by the general state of the firm's finances. The need for cash may arise directly from the cost of a routine renewal of plant or assets quite unconnected with the project under discussion, but if this project is, in a sense, optional, while the continuation of the firm's main business is not regarded as optional, it is the decision to go ahead with the optional project that makes the subsequent equity issue necessary. If I decide to fly to the Riviera to get some sun, and pay for the air ticket by borrowing the money my wife has saved to pay the rates, my need to seek an overdraft when the final demand for the rates arrives is a consequence of my Mediterranean holiday, for which I had not budgeted, and not of the rates, for which my wife had not only budgeted but provided.

This homely example can be used to show the principles on which a financing plan is made. Suppose my wife keeps money put by for rates and other household contingencies in a Post Office savings account bearing interest at 2½% (tax free because she gets less than £15 a year). Suppose the net-of-tax cost of a bank overdraft is ½% per month, and that it takes me six months to replace the amount spent on my trip, but the rates are not due for three months. Then collectively my wife and I, who may be regarded as shareholders in the same firm, can gain by foregoing interest at the rate of 2½% per year for 3 months, and paying interest at 6% a year for a further three months, instead of receiving 2½% for three months and paying 6% on the same sum for six months.

If my intention is to pay for the trip in a lump sum after six months, say with some back-pay due in six months time, the cost involves borrowing a sum of money for 3 months at 5/24ths of 1% per month (=2½% p.a.) and refinancing the amount owing at the end of that time for a further 3 months at ½% per month. If on the other hand I save approximately one-sixth of the price of the ticket each month the advantage gained is greater, since the higher rate will apply to only half the original cost of the ticket in the fourth month, and one-sixth of it in the last month.

Timing of investment

For a firm planning its operations over years rather than months, the timing of investments and new issues is of great importance. If an investment costing £1 million can be financed by loans and internal funds until half its cost has been recouped in gross profits, the new equity issue which eventually becomes necessary will be only £0·5 million, perhaps in some years' time. From the point of view of the shareholders at the time the project is planned, the need to raise £500,000 new equity in a future year is much less formidable than a requirement to raise £1 million at once. A project that would be turned down out of hand if it meant raising £1 million new equity this year might well be accepted if the cost were modified to be three years' loss of interest on £1 million (reducing) followed by an issue of £500,000 new equity.

This rather spoils the simplicity of the models we started with, since if the cost of capital varies over the life of a project it is no longer possible to set out the cash flows attributable and bring them to their present values by discounting at a single rate. Nor is knowing 'the' rate of return necessarily going to help. For various reasons it is often easiest to calculate terminal values in these circumstances.[1] Terminal values are calculated by compounding amounts forward to a fixed date in the future, instead of discounting back to the present.

Suppose that a project, whose cost we will call 100, can be financed initially by a mixture of loans and internal funds whose net cost, after corporation tax, is 6% per year. At the end of the third year a sum equal to the initial cost will be required for other purposes—it may be assumed to have been 'borrowed' from the firm's depreciation reserve—and a new equity issue of which the after-tax cost is estimated to be 10% will be needed to finance the balance of cost outstanding. (For the sake of simplicity we assume that dividends are not affected in this period, which is reasonable enough, considering that there has as yet been no recourse to new equity finance.) We assume that all gross profits accruing from the investment (before depreciation but after tax) can be invested temporarily to earn 5% after corporation tax—a return slightly less than the 6% average cost of internal funds, etc., diverted to the project. The investment is expected to earn nothing in the first year, but to show returns (*before* depreciation but *after* corporation tax) of 30 per year for the next five years, after which it becomes worthless.

Since the size of the equity issue required after three years is affected by profits earned during that period, the two halves of the project's six-year life must be considered separately. After the first 3 years the initial cost of 100 will have accumulated at 6% to 119. Profits of 60 earned in years 2 and 3 will be worth approximately 62 (with interest at 5% on the first year's profit). Therefore the amount to be financed will be 57, and on our assumptions this will have to be raised by a new equity issue. (The fact that it is not a round sum is neither here nor there, since new shares in established companies are offered for sale not at their par value but at a figure equal to the market value before the issue less a discount calculated to ensure that the issue is taken up. If, as is probable, the issue is a 'rights' issue offered in the first place to existing shareholders, there is likely to be a further discount designed to enable those shareholders who cannot take up their entitlement to sell their 'rights' for a sum that compensates them for the fact that future profits have to be shared with outsiders who are acquiring their shares on relatively favourable terms—see chapter 6.) On our assumptions, the issue price will be such that a return of 10% after corporation tax is required to make the investment worth while from the point of view of the existing shareholders in the company.

At the end of year 3, therefore, when the temporary finance ceases to be available, we have to earn 10% after corporation tax on a net investment of 57 to make the venture worth while for the shareholders. Prospective post-tax returns are 30 in each of the three succeeding years. We can establish that the return exceeds 10% either by discounting the returns at 10% and subtracting 57 (present value method) or compounding both the investment (57) and the returns to the terminal year at an interest rate of 10%. Either way the investment shows a profit, having net present value (at the end of year 3) of (75−57)=18, and net terminal value (99−76)=23. The net terminal value is greater than the net present value because the latter is the discounted value of the net profits, over and above the minimum needed to remunerate capital, while the former expresses the value of the same net profits accumulated for some years at compound interest. Obviously, therefore, net terminal values cannot be compared directly with net present values, and if priorities have to be assigned to a number of projects they must all be brought to a common base year value before rational choices can be made.

This chapter illustrates a further disadvantage of using the rate of return as an investment criterion. Certainly, if the *marginal* cost of new equity funds is 10% after corporation tax, any investment which offers a rate of return exceeding 10% will be worth considering. But if some part of the finance can be found from loans or internal funds, even if only on a temporary basis, investments yielding appreciably less than 10% may be well worth while from the shareholders' point of view. To establish whether or not this is so, however, a financing plan is necessary, and several different interest (discount) rates may have to be used to deal with all the complexities that arise in practice. The common notion that it is better to use rate of return than present value (or terminal value) when the cost of capital is not known is a fallacy, since it is only when the cost of capital is known that rate of return can be used to distinguish between those investments that are worth while and those that are not. When the relevant cost of capital lies somewhere between a minimum given by the cost of loan finance and the return obtainable on depreciation funds and other reserves invested through the market, and a maximum given by the cost of new outside equity finance, it is always necessary to know how a project yielding something between the two extremes would be financed before its worthwhileness can be assessed. And making a financing plan necessarily involves calculating net present or terminal values.

NOTES

[1] J. T. S. Porterfield: *Investment Decisions and Capital Costs*, pp. 38-41.

9

Investment programming I: Choice between investments

So far we have discussed the problem of assessing the worthwhileness of individual investments on certain assumptions about the availability and cost of finance. In this and the following chapter we shall mention some of the questions that arise in connection with the compilation of a capital programme involving a number of projects to be undertaken over a period of years. There are two main aspects. First, it is necessary to have some means of ranking projects in an order of preference, so that choice can be made between investments that are in some sense alternative to one another. Secondly, given that it may be impossible to find a single interest (discount) rate that correctly expresses the cost of capital at all times and for any size of programme, we have to decide how many of the projects that pass the first screening test (in that they offer returns greater than whatever minimum value we assign to the cost of capital, and are not inferior to any known alternatives) should be included in the current investment budget, and if necessary assign priorities in time. An iterative process may sometimes be needed, because we cannot know the marginal cost of capital until we have at least an idea of the size of programme to be financed, but we need a discount rate of some sort to carry out the initial screening process and find out how many projects would be worth undertaking if no financial constraints were imposed.

To start with, then, it will be useful to evaluate all projects put forward for consideration by finding their net present or terminal values, using a single discount rate corresponding to the estimated marginal cost of finance assuming that no new equity capital has to be raised from outside. As we have seen, this is a relatively simple concept, since it is usually possible to get some idea of the terms on which new loan capital can be had in quantities that will not add significantly to the risk premium demanded by lenders, and the directors may be presumed to have formed some judgment about prospective returns obtainable on marginal employment of any internal funds that may be available for investment. For illustrative purposes we shall assume that the directors' best guess is that projects that can be financed without recourse to new outside equity will be worth considering if they offer prospective returns exceeding 7% after corporation tax.

We begin, then, by calculating the net present value, at 7% discount, of all the investments put up for consideration. In this first screening process any investment that has positive present value at 7% (that is, any investment offering a return of more than 7% after corporation tax) gets by in principle, though the directors, whose duties include exercising judgment as to the risks that are acceptable, may at this stage reject any project whose prospective profitability seems to them inadequate in relation to the sum invested and the risk and uncertainty involved. As risks outside the insurable class cannot be expressed in terms of numerical probability, this is essentially an exercise in entrepreneurial judgment, and not strictly a function of the investment analyst acting in his professional capacity. No precise rules can be laid down, since in the nature of things some projects will appear more risky than others, some managers are more optimistic than others, and some firms can afford to lose more money than others.

While the investment analyst cannot always be expected to quantify risks in a way that enables him to present outcomes in the form of what are sometimes called 'risk-adjusted returns', he can and should be expected to assist managerial judgment by bringing out as clearly as possible what are the critical variables, and what difference is made to the outcome of any project by varying the assumptions made about these variables. The present value of an investment may then appear not as a single figure, but as a range of possible values within which one figure is as probable as another. If all the values are positive the risk of loss is plainly low, and the project may pass the first screening test even if it is only just profitable. If on the other hand the range includes negative values, it will be for management to decide whether the risks are acceptable. The risk of loss is most likely to be acceptable if the prospective losses are not large enough to cause serious difficulty or embarrassment, and are matched by the expectation of attractive profits if things go reasonably well.

Incompatible alternatives

Having eliminated those projects which are insufficiently profitable, and those which appear too risky, the next step is to choose between any investments that are, for one reason or another, incompatible with each other. Investments may be mutually exclusive for technical reasons—e.g. because the firm's physical resources will not permit both to be undertaken at once. Typically there will be a number of constraints applying during any reasonably short period, including factory floor space, machine capacity, and managerial and technical expertise. Or there may be incompatibilities at the marketing end. If you are planning a campaign to convert gardeners to plastic watering cans you may think it inadvisable to build a new plant to make stainless steel watering cans. The simplest case of all is that in which a case has been established for installing one new boiler and furnace capable of delivering steam at a certain rate for use in the firm's own processes, and if a coal-fired boiler is installed there will be no point in contemplating one fired by gas or oil as well.

The general rule in such cases is that an investment with higher present value than an alternative is preferable to that alternative, given that neither involves an unacceptable degree of risk and that both are within the firm's budgetary resources. Here again, though, managerial judgment may be called in to settle the issue. If there is a large difference in cost between two alternatives, but comparatively little difference between their net present values, the cheaper alternative may be chosen even though its present value is slightly less. Most people would rather invest £5,000 in a project with net present value £600 than spend £25,000 on an alternative with net present value £850. Money is never in unlimited supply, and the future is always uncertain. But this sentiment must not be generalized into a belief that what matters primarily is the ratio of present value to cost. An investment with a present value of £200 is twice as profitable as one with present value £100, after allowing for all capital charges including a return equal to the estimated opportunity cost of the capital required in each case.

Overall constraints

There is one circumstance, however, in which an investment with lower present value than an alternative will rationally be chosen, without invoking any judgments about risk, etc. Suppose that a prior managerial decision has been taken that no new outside equity will be raised in the next three years. Then the investment programme for this period is made subject to an overriding financial constraint, since the total cost in any year may not exceed the internal resources available plus any borrowing that may be sanctioned. If the total cost of the projects that pass the initial screening test exceeds the finance available, choosing a more costly project in preference to a cheaper alternative will automatically exclude some other profitable investment. It does not necessarily follow that, because alternative A is more profitable than alternative B, and both A and B are in themselves more profitable than F, whose cost is equal to the difference between the costs of A and B and which could be included in this year's programme if the cheaper alternative B were chosen in preference to A, a programme consisting of A, C, D, and E only will be more profitable than one comprising B, C, D, E, and F. All depends on whether the present value of F is greater or less than the difference between the present values of A and B. Thus before choice can be made between A and B, comparison has to be made between the present value of A, and that of (B plus F), which is the real alternative to A. (If a relaxation of the financial constraint can be foreseen in the near future with reasonable certainty, it may be better to compare the advantage A has over B with the disadvantage of postponing F until the time when finance will be available for it if A is chosen now in preference to B.)

Financial constraints are not at all uncommon. In many large firms decision-making is decentralized both to encourage enterprise and profit-consciousness in subsidiary or divisional managements and to leave central management free to concentrate on major policy issues instead of spending its time appraising in detail the very large numbers of investment projects of all kinds and sizes that are likely to be considered within a major industrial group in a normal year. Sometimes cost limits are fixed for various levels; perhaps projects costing up to £1,000 may be authorized by branch managers, up to £10,000 by divisional managers, and up to £100,000 by the boards of subsidiary companies, while everything costing more than £100,000 has to be considered by the board of the parent company. But unless the cost limits are small in relation to the firm's financial resources, control may require a restriction on the total amount of expenditure that can be authorized at any level below the main board in any year or other accounting period. Therefore in addition to, or instead of, cost limits on individual projects, management below the top echelon may have to work within capital budgets fixed in advance without knowledge of the proposals that will come forward for consideration during the period. Obviously there is an arbitrariness in this process, but a certain amount of arbitrariness may be preferable to the lack of effective control that is apparent if subordinate management is allowed to sanction any project that appears likely to yield more than some pre-determined rate of return, or over-centralization of decision-making, which can have paralysing effects on subordinate management and put intolerable strain on top management.

Naturally, any major change in circumstances that seems to call for a revision of capital budgets can be brought to the attention of central management, who can, if they think fit, revise investment budgets either by re-allocating resources among divisions/subsidiaries or by deciding to raise additional capital from outside. But decisions as to how and when to raise outside finance have to be reserved for central management, except perhaps to the extent that subsidiary companies may be able to arrange additional overdraft finance with their bankers. If new equity capital will be required, the most careful and detailed consideration of the long-term effects on the position of the existing shareholders is necessary before a decision can be made. New loan or debenture issues usually cause less difficulty, but central management will still want to consider the pros and cons of creating more prior charges (interest and/or amortization obligations that take precedence over dividend payments) before authorizing an increase in loans or debentures.

The process of allocating resources optimally within an overall constraint is often called sub-optimizing. Sub-optimizing has many facets, of which we have so far mentioned only one—the possibility that choosing the better of two incompatible alternatives may, if the budget is fixed and the 'inferior' alternative is less costly, exclude a third project which, taken together with the 'inferior' alternative, may be more profitable than the 'superior' alternative on its own. Another problem that often arises in a sub-optimizing situation is that of assigning priorities in time to the components of an investment programme that cannot be accommodated within the capital budget laid down. In simple language, what should be done first?

Priorities in time

The object of ranking projects in an order of preference in time is to find the programme whose present value is highest within the constraint imposed by an upper limit on the amount of capital that can be spent in any one year. The investments that should receive priority are not necessarily those which have highest present value or rate of return on the assumption that all projects passing the profitability test can be and are carried out without delay. There are basically two reasons for this. First, some interdependence exists between many investment projects and between the different activities of a firm. Some projects are complementary to others, and there is often a logical order in which schemes should be carried out, irrespective of how profitable each would be considered separately. The profitability of the whole may be greater than the sum of the parts, but the several parts may, for technological or marketing reasons, for example, have to be done in a certain sequence if the best overall result is to be achieved. The financial constraint itself may be eased, or at any rate prevented from growing more restrictive, if projects that begin to earn profits quickly are given priority over those with longer gestation periods. (This is particularly important if what is constrained is borrowing rather than capital expenditure.)

Secondly, some investments can be postponed with little or no effect on their eventual profitability; some may even gain from postponement, though this is not a reason for postponing them if capital is available at a cost lower than the estimated return if they are done now. But if something has to be postponed, a project that will be more profitable if started later is obviously a better candidate than something which is urgently needed, either to fit in with other activities or projects, or because a lucrative market may be lost to a competitor if a new product is delayed. In a competitive situation time is often of the essence, and at the opposite end of the scale from investments which become more profitable the longer they are delayed—perhaps because they involve replacing equipment that is still usable but growing more expensive and unreliable every year—are things which must be done at once to be worth doing at all. For example, a firm that has an acknowledged technical lead in some field may derive considerable advantage from its position, and be prepared to spend quite a lot of money to ensure that no potential competitor is encouraged to encroach on it. Particularly in oligopolistic situations, a firm that allows rivals to increase their market share at its expense may find it difficult to recover lost ground later on. The general term 'defensive investment' is applied to expenditure that is necessary, not so much to increase profits, as to guard against profitability being eroded, and erosion is a process that does not stand still.

Interdependence

Simple examples of complementarity and interdependence are easily found. If you have an integrated steelworks, and transport costs between your location and the nearest source of supply of semi-finished steel of suitable quality make it uneconomic to use steel made outside the plant in your rolling or re-rolling mills, adding more rolling capacity will only unbalance the plant and (probably) reduce profits unless steelmaking capacity is also enlarged. A transport undertaking must have maintenance facilities before it can expand its vehicle fleet, unless the work can be satisfactorily done by an outside contractor. These are fairly simple examples, and it could be said that it should be easy enough to consider investments that are related to each other in these ways as complete units of investment rather than as separate components of a programme. But if we consider the complexity of a large multi-product firm in the chemical industry, for example, and the amount of detailed planning that must go into its future development, it should not be difficult to appreciate that a programme that is too big to be carried through in the current planning period ought not to be cut down to a suitable size by the crude method of postponing all the projects with rates of return below r%, or with present value less than X at i%. The whole organization might become unbalanced, and profits adversely affected, if investment planning followed such a rule of thumb. Basically the problem is one of inter-dependence, both between the various divisions (or subsidiaries) of the parent organization, and between individual investment projects. These two sorts of inter-dependence might be termed institutional and technological interdependence, and both have to be allowed for in drawing up an investment programme, or adapting an existing programme to meet the requirements of a changed situation or a rise in the cost of finance.

The object of keeping a balance between different activities or divisions is primarily to make the best use of plant, labour, and management capacity possessed by the firm. Within each division a balance has to be kept between materials supply, production, and marketing if full efficiency is to be maintained. In addition to all this a firm may wish to include some low-risk (and therefore possibly low-profit) investments in its programme, balanced by some high-profit (probably more risky) projects. Cutting out the lowest yielding projects might leave the firm with an unacceptable proportion of high-risk investments even if no inter-dependence existed. Or a multi-product firm may as a matter of policy aim at retaining some minimum market share in all its spheres of interest, unless its management decides that some activity is becoming so hopelessly unprofitable that it should be abandoned altogether. This conduct can be rationalized in conditions of imperfect competition, since the influence which an individual producer is able to exert on prices and selling conditions may be related to his relative importance in the market. Moreover, distributors, and suppliers of materials and components, may make arrangements with large producers which they would not willingly extend to their smaller competitors. If there are important economies of scale at any point in the productive or distributive process, a reduction in market share may be attended with disproportionate penalties in the longer run.

Incompatible alternatives with different lives

Even in the absence of a budget constraint, the simple criteria of present value or rate of return may fail to give a clear answer when incompatible (mutually exclusive) alternatives have to be compared over different periods. A durable investment may have higher present value than a less durable alternative simply because it is more durable, and so goes on generating profits longer. But it is not necessarily superior to a series of shorter-lived but cheaper investments that will fulfil the same purpose. Rate of return is not affected by durability in the same way, but as we have seen in chapter 4 we have to know the incremental rate of return in order to compare two or more alternative investments with each other, and the result of subtracting one cash flow from another may be an irregular series of inflows and outflows for which a unique and meaningful rate of return is not easily found. (Large firms employing skilled mathematical programmers with access to computer time will solve such problems easily enough, but it may be some time before all investment appraisal in this and other countries is carried out by such highly skilled analysts. Moreover even the greatest minds can make mistakes, and simplicity is always desirable where it can be had without sacrifice of efficiency because it is likely to lead to fewer mistakes, or at least to make mistakes more readily spotted and corrected.)

Present value can be used for these comparisons if it is assumed that the less durable alternative can be repeated, so that the long-term alternative can be compared with a series of shorter-lived investments extending over the same time span. If it seems appropriate, an assumption about future technical progress can be made, the second and subsequent versions of the short-lived alternative being credited with lower costs (outflows) or higher net receipts (inflows) than preceding models. In other words, allowance can be made for rising capital productivity over time just as allowance should be made for rising wages due fundamentally to rising labour productivity when comparing more and less labour-intensive projects.

If the probable life of the less durable alternative happens to divide exactly into that of the more durable, the exercise is straightforward enough. Otherwise a good approximation can usually be got by considering residual values—there may be some arbitrariness, but the present value of the difference between residual values calculated in different ways will seldom be large unless the period of comparison is short. However, a useful short cut exists. Using the same interest/discount rate as that used to calculate present values, the present value of each alternative can be expressed as an annuity extending over a number of years equal to the expected life of the asset. The project with the higher annuity value calculated in this way is the one which will have the higher present value if all alternatives are compared over the same length of time.

For example, suppose a durable investment (D) with a prospective earning life of 18 years has to be compared with a shorter-lived alternative (S) that will fulfil the same function but need renewing after 9 years. Let the cost of capital be 8% in each case, and assume that the net present values at 8% discount are 300 for D and 200 for S. Since the present value at 8% of 200 in year 9 is 100 in year 0, S undertaken in year 0 and renewed in year 9 will have present value in year 0 of 300, the same as D undertaken in year 0, if other things remain unchanged. Thus a present value calculation extending over 18 years shows D and S as equally attractive, assuming that S can be renewed in year 9. The same result is obtained by converting the original present values of 300 and 200 into annuities extending over 18 years and 9 years respectively, using the same discount rate of 8%. At this rate the capital value of an annuity for 18 years is found by multiplying the annuity by 9·372, and that of an annuity lasting for 9 years by multiplying by 6·247. Simple arithmetic shows that $\frac{300}{9\cdot372}=32=\frac{200}{6\cdot247}$. In practice choice would be influenced in favour of S if capital were scarce or if technical progress could be expected to result in the replacement for S being cheaper than or technically superior to the original S. On the other hand D might be preferred if it were less labour-intensive than S in an economy where wages tended to rise faster than other input prices.

10

Investment programming II: The size of the programme

After insufficiently profitable projects and inferior alternatives have been eliminated by the screening process discussed in the last chapter we are left with a list of investments, all of which it would be nice to undertake if enough finance were available at a cost not exceeding the interest/discount rate used in the screening process. Some firms will find that internal resources plus permissible borrowing are adequate to finance all the investment they wish to carry out. For these firms, planning the investment budget is a relatively simple operation, and it is rightly said that the difficult part of the work is predicting the outcomes, not ranking them. Others, however, will be obliged to choose between rejecting—or indefinitely postponing—investment projects that are attractive in their own right and likely to increase the profitability, prestige, and influence of the firm, and raising new outside equity capital, expensive though this often is.

Since the cost of new equity tends to increase with the amount—because more stock has to be sold to outsiders—there is no single figure, even in principle, which can be used as a cut-off or test rate for determining the optimum size of programme. Optimization is a complex and time-consuming process that cannot be satisfactorily dealt with in a non-mathematical introductory textbook. A financing plan has to be attached to each size of programme, and the increase in the marginal cost of finance that is likely to go with adoption of a bigger programme may change the ranking of projects, since the order of preference that emerged after the initial screening process is in part a consequence of the discount rate used in that exercise. If the programme contemplated requires a proportion of external financing that raises the marginal cost of finance above the discount rate used for initial screening and ranking, it is necessary to go back and check that all the projects in the programme have positive present value at the new and higher discount rate, and that alternatives that appeared inferior at the original discount rate are not superior at the new and higher rate, which will of course tend to favour projects of a less capital-intensive kind.

Priorities in time may also be changed when the marginal cost of finance alters, and it is to be expected that a rise in the cost of capital will increase the advantage of giving more priority to investments likely to yield substantial cash returns in the early years, since these receipts can be used to finance later projects, reducing the amount of new equity finance required over a finite period.

Management may also have to take a view about the time preferences of shareholders. Possibly holding down dividends for a time would enable a larger programme to be financed without a new equity issue beyond the resources of the existing shareholders; at the very least, more internal financing must mean less external finance. In the long run this will be to the advantage of the existing shareholders. But since the market is usually thought to overvalue shares offering high immediate dividends in relation to shares with better long-run prospects, the shareholder who does not want to wait for his money may be prejudiced if he sells his holding with the object of using the money to acquire shares in a firm whose directors are more open-handed. But time-preference, like the acceptable degree of risk, is a matter of opinion.

It should be obvious that all investment incentives offered by the government need to be taken into account when deciding how much investment can be financed during any period of time. Investment grants and other cash subsidies not only increase the return on shareholders' capital but may also permit a proportion of debt (fixed-interest) financing that would be imprudent if the company could not rely with certainty on recovering 20% or more of qualifying outlays with 1 to 1½ years, over and above any profits that might have been earned. It is usually easier to borrow for relatively short periods against the security of a payment due from some official source than it is to borrow for longer periods, or even for short periods when punctual repayment is contingent on expectations about profits being fulfilled.

Initial allowances and other tax incentives such as higher annual depreciation allowances also increase liquidity, by reducing taxes payable in the years immediately following investment outlays. Here again, assuming the company is making taxable profits somewhere, an immediate financial benefit is felt that does not depend on the earnings of a particular investment and that can properly be taken into account when arranging short-term loan finance. Or, to look at the matter another way, the knowledge of reliefs which the company will be entitled to claim when tax on profits currently being earned falls due to be paid, reduces the provision for future tax which has to be made out of current profits, and makes a corresponding amount of additional finance available for investment. As we saw in chapter 8, even if a new issue eventually becomes necessary, if it can be deferred until the investment has earned enough to repay some of its cost, the financing cost will be much reduced. Large companies in the U.S.A. and Canada have developed means for economizing cash into a fine art, and all companies whose investment is limited by shortage of liquid resources could study this aspect of management with advantage.

In chapter 9 reference was made to the ordering of priorities in time. When investment is limited by finance available there will often be a case for giving some priority not only to projects that offer immediate or early cash returns, but also to those that attract investment grants or other cash assistance, such as regional subsidies on factory buildings; provided taxable profits are already being earned, projects that qualify for initial allowances or relatively high annual allowances in the first years will also help out the cash position.

11
Public investment

Discounted cash flow methods of investment appraisal can be and are used in the public sector. Indeed the use of these methods by nationalized industries is specifically recommended in the 1967 White Paper,[1] and the technique is also the basis of cost-benefit analysis, which will be discussed in chapter 13 of this book. In so far as public trading bodies are motivated by commercial considerations there may be little difference between their approach to an investment problem and that of a private firm. Two important qualifications, however, must be made. In the first place public undertakings do not issue ordinary shares, and they obtain their loan capital either by market issues backed by an Exchequer guarantee or by direct borrowing from the Exchequer. This makes an important difference to the conditions on which capital is available. Private firms, as we have seen, are normally faced with an upward sloping supply schedule of funds. They may have substantial liquid reserves, in the form of cash or marketable securities earning comparatively low rates of return, and they may reckon to add to these internal funds not only the amounts provided each year for depreciation, but substantial appropriations out of current profits. At present in this country private firms gain tax advantages by ploughing back profits, since income tax and surtax are charged only on profits distributed to shareholders. These internal funds can be supplemented up to a point by the proceeds of new issues of loan stocks and debentures, which are relatively cheap sources of capital because loan interest can be deducted from profits before computing liability for corporation tax, and the relative absence of risk makes investors willing to accept lower returns on the loan stocks of 'sound' business concerns than they look for on equities. The limitation on a company's ability to raise new loan capital is that this relative freedom from risk would be compromised if loan interest came to absorb too high a proportion of profits, since a company's ability to meet payments punctually might become suspect. The security for the capital, too, might be difficult to find, since the value of a company as a successful going concern is normally a good deal higher than the break-up value of its assets, which is what holders of secured loan stocks and debentures have to fall back on if the company goes into liquidation. Shareholders too would see their position deteriorating if prior charges such as loan interest came to account for too high a proportion of profits.

When internal resources and loan capital are exhausted, private firms can raise further funds only by issuing new equity shares, and as we saw in chapter 6 the cost of this is higher, and increases with the amount to be raised if, as is likely, both the proportion subscribed by existing shareholders and the price at which the issue has to be marketed fall as the size of the issue increases. (Up to a point, however, this tendency for costs to rise may be offset by lower *ad valorem* issuing costs.) At some stage the marginal cost of raising further capital may become prohibitive, and this explains why overall budget constraints are not uncommon.

A public undertaking is in a different position. If it gets its loan capital from the Exchequer it can borrow as much as the government is willing to lend at interest rates fixed by government decisions. These rates may reflect current yields on marketable government securities, but the government is not obliged to raise any or all of its capital requirements by market issues; it can, and to a large extent does, rely on taxation to finance its requirements. If a public body issues its own securities, backed by a government guarantee, market conditions may have more effect on the amounts that can be raised at any given rate of interest. But the gilt-edged market is very wide relative to the marginal requirements of individual industries, and the monetary authorities can usually take steps to facilitate the success of a particular issue if they choose to do so. In the last resort it is likely in practice that the government would make temporary finance available from its own resources to a nationalized industry or other public body unable to raise finance in the market for an investment programme that had been approved by the Minister responsible. Thus public undertakings will usually be able to rely on obtaining external finance needed for approved investment programmes at fixed rates of interest which are likely to vary only gradually if market conditions change.

The essential condition for obtaining finance for public investment is that the investing body should be able to satisfy the appropriate government department that its capital programme is a proper use of national resources. In order to do so it may have to demonstrate that the investments proposed are likely to be profitable in the financial sense. At one time it was assumed that a prospective return exceeding the rate of interest on government loans would suffice for this purpose, but requirements have recently grown more stringent, and in the 1967 White Paper a 'test rate of discount' of 8% is recommended. The reasons for this will be discussed in the next chapter.

Not all public investments are expected to show profits in the monetary sense. The Victoria Tube is unlikely to earn much of a return on capital directly, but its construction was justified by a calculation that it would be worth while because of the reduction in road congestion that it would bring.[2] This decision required the application of cost-benefit analysis, a brief introduction to which will be found in chapter 13. A willingness to consider investments which are not financially profitable in themselves, but which appear to be desirable on social or wider economic grounds is the second way in which public investment criteria differ from those employed in the private sector. The directors of a private company are appointed by the shareholders, to whom they are responsible for the proper conduct of the business, and even if the majority shareholders of a private company contemplated building an unprofitable underground railway line for the public good they would probably be challenged in the courts by minority shareholders on the ground that such an undertaking was not a proper use of the company's resources because it was not for the benefit of the shareholders.

The factors which may be taken into account in deciding whether or not a public investment project is a use of resources which is for the benefit of the community are many and various. Among them are road congestion, safety, security of essential supplies and services, the efficient use of resources (especially labour), and regional policy in its many aspects. A private firm may discharge surplus labour having regard only to the compensation it is legally required to pay, but the public interest requires us to ask if and when labour discharged by public undertakings will be re-employed, if the true long-run economic costs and benefits are to be established. When investments are undertaken by non-trading bodies, such as education authorities or hospital boards, the enumeration and (if possible) valuation of social costs and benefits is the only means of assessing value for money in quantitative terms.

Investment programming may be even more important in the public sector than in private industry. For all but the largest private firms the field of choice is limited, and decisions about financing can be taken from year to year in the light of market conditions and internal resources available. Profits are often rather volatile, and a successful trading year may both generate a large increase in profits available for reinvestment and create conditions propitious for a new issue, enabling considerably more investment to be financed than could prudently have been committed when sales and profits were at lower levels. Conversely, private investment sometimes has to be cut back fairly sharply because finance is not available on reasonable terms.

Public investment is largely financed by the Exchequer, and the total annual borrowing requirements of nationalized industries and local authorities are so large that the government is bound to ask for forecasts extending several years ahead. In the absence of such forecasts intelligent budgeting would be very difficult. Approval of programmes for the next financial year is normally sought well before the end of the year preceding, and provisional approval may be given as much as two years ahead. As circumstances change, additional investments may be sanctioned if a case is made out for them, and projects that have been approved may for one reason or another not get carried out in the year in which they were programmed. When pressure on national resources is extreme, government may call for cuts or deferments in programmes. But these changes are usually marginal.

When a very large global sum has to be allocated in advance between a number of undertakings covering a field as extensive as the public sector of the British economy, which in 1966 comprised 47% of all fixed investment in the economy,[3] intelligent long-range programming is clearly desirable if the best use is to be made of resources. In principle the object of such an exercise should be to find the programme for the whole public sector whose present value is greatest at the discount rate chosen (see next chapter). In practice this is probably impossible with our existing institutions and techniques, and a certain amount of sub-optimizing is inevitable. But many of the investing bodies in the public sector are themselves very large, and complex programming techniques will be needed even if our objective is limited to optimizing industry by industry.

NOTES

[1] Cmnd. 3437, paragraph 8.

[2] C. D. Foster and M. E. Beesley: 'Estimating the Social Benefit of constructing an Underground Railway in London' in *Journal of the Royal Statistical Society*, vol. 126, Part 1, 1963.

[3] *National Income and Expenditure*, 1967, Table 55.

12

The cost of capital invested in the public sector

There has been considerable controversy over the rate at which public undertakings should discount future receipts and costs when appraising investment. The various nationalization Acts in this country broadly required industries to meet the demand for their products and services in the most efficient way and to conduct their affairs so that they would at least break even over time, and make some contribution to reserves. It was commonly assumed that investment needed to earn only enough to cover amortization and interest at a rate resembling the current yield of government securities, or the rate at which the industry borrowed from the Exchequer.

Such a criterion is unsatisfactory for two reasons. The rate of interest on government or government-guaranteed securities is a riskless rate, but the business of a nationalized industry is not inherently less risky than that of a large, well-established private firm. The degree of monopoly possessed by many public undertakings, and the likelihood that demand for such things as fuel, public transport, and telephones can be forecast more accurately than can demand for many goods and services produced in the private sector, may well suggest comparison with the least risky classes of private business rather than with average risk business. But not even the least risky private firm can command the whole of its capital requirements at gilt-edged rates of interest, and it is impossible to justify such a degree of discrimination in favour of public enterprise in a mixed economy with a high level of employment. A decision to nationalize an industry does not imply that it should necessarily become more capital-intensive.

Another reason for regarding gilt-edged rates as an invalid criterion is that, risk apart, the capital invested in the public sector is not raised wholly (or even mainly) by market borrowing. In 1966 gross fixed capital formation by local authorities and public corporations in the United Kingdom totalled £2,777 million. The undistributed income of these bodies, before providing for depreciation and stock appreciation, was £1,059 million. Net public sector sales of financial assets of all kinds totalled £778 million.[1] A large proportion of the finance provided by the Exchequer is found from taxation, and the market yield of government securities at any time cannot be taken as even a good approximation to the true marginal cost of capital. How much higher interest rates would be if all capital requirements of the public sector were raised by market issues of stock is impossible to guess, but it is quite certain that such a policy, even if it proved feasible, would drive interest rates much higher than they now are. (It is worth recalling that interest rates doubled during the First World War, mainly because of heavy government borrowing. In the Second World War, when different techniques of financing were employed, interest rates were actually forced down.)

Opportunity: cost of capital

If public investment is financed by withdrawing through taxation money which might have been used—and which, having been withdrawn from consumption could in principle be used—to finance additional private investment, the real marginal cost of the capital invested in the public sector will be its opportunity cost, defined as the return that might have been earned by a marginal addition to private investment. In the nature of things this is difficult to quantify with any precision. As we have seen in earlier chapters, the supply curve of capital to a private firm is seldom if ever horizontal, and investment grants and other incentives complicate the picture further because they affect different types of investment unequally. A return before tax that might be acceptable to a manufacturing firm in a development area, with ample liquid reserves and little opportunity to employ them profitably outside the company, would be hopelessly inadequate in the case of a project that did not qualify for an investment grant and would require a new issue of equity capital to finance it.

However, we are probably justified in disregarding both these extremes. The best that can be done in practice is to find a figure that is reasonably representative of the minimum return on new investment that might be acceptable in a low-risk category when finance could be provided from loans or internal sources. In chapter 7 we argued that returns of 7% to 10% after corporation tax might be required to give investors returns which made them content to hold wealth in the form of risk-bearing securities (equities) rather than in fixed-interest bonds. This, if the argument is correct, will be the minimum return required on the proportion of the cost of an investment financed by shareholders' capital, after taking account of any grants or subsidies received from the government, including investment grants, and also of any favourable 'gearing' that may be possible if part of the cost can be raised by an issue of loan capital. These latter factors vary so much between individual investments that it is impossible to fix on one figure to express the gross return before taxes and grants that will correspond even broadly to that required in the private sector to yield 7% to 10% on shareholders' capital after corporate taxes and grants. However the 8% test discount rate for nationalized industries promulgated in a recent White Paper lies roughly at the centre of a range of returns which, on different assumptions about the proportion of expenditure qualifying for investment grants, etc., would yield net-of-tax returns of the order required. A calculation made by Mr J. M. Barber shows that an investment of 1000 yielding 149 p.a. gross for 10 years (=8% d.c.f. return) would show the following rates of return after corporation tax at 40%:

With investment allowance of 45% (development area)	14%
With investment allowance of 25%	10%
With no investment allowance but 30% initial allowance	6%

(This apparently paradoxical result that the return after tax in the first two cases is higher than the return before tax is due to the present value of the investment grant being (typically) greater than the present value of the tax eventually payable on a fairly low-profit investment.)

Despite these uncertainties, the principle that the cost of capital invested in the public sector is its opportunity cost, based on returns that might be expected at the margin if the capital were invested in the private sector, is extremely important. If investible resources are allocated in such a way that prospective returns at the margin are the same in both public and private sectors, there will be no case for arguing that total wealth could be increased by restraining public investment in order to 'make room for' more private investment, and consequently no case for restraining or cutting back public investment unless equal restraints are imposed on private investment. No other criterion fulfils this condition.

Time preference

Several economists[2] have recommended the use of a discount rate based on social time preference to appraise public investments. In an ideal world with a perfect capital market there would be no difference between a rate based on time-preference and one derived from opportunity-cost. The inducement to save would be the expectation of the risk-adjusted return on investment, which in the perfect market assumed would be the same for all firms. In the real world conditions are somewhat different. The marginal social return to investment may be higher than the return received by private individuals supplying funds through the market, because of taxation. The volume of saving forthcoming in expectation of any given return may be affected by changes in the distribution of income, which is also affected by taxation. The supply schedule of capital facing an individual firm may slope upwards quite steeply, for reasons explained in chapters 6–8. (Note that this has nothing to do with the intrinsic risks of the particular investment projects for which a firm may contemplate raising capital.) And capital needed for public investment is not raised wholly, or even mainly, by a market process in which interest rates find their own level as the result of a competitive scramble for funds. So we are left in a situation very different from the idealized picture alluded to above, and it is not possible to demonstrate any connection between the social time-preference rate and the opportunity-cost of capital.

This brings us at once to a formidable difficulty in the way of making use of the concept of social time-preference, since in the situation that actually exists it is impossible to find any criteria by which the time preference rate could be determined, and the practical usefulness of the concept is obviously much diminished if it cannot be measured. It might even be argued that, since the total supply of savings is determined at the margin by governmental decisions about the balance between expenditure and taxation which define the level of public saving, the marginal productivity of capital at the full-employment level of investment is as good a measure of the social time-preference rate as can be found. If society collectively wished to save more in order to enjoy the benefits of more investment, an argument might run, the government could gain popularity by imposing more taxation and taking steps to encourage investment. If it is representative of popular opinion, the point where it decides to stop restraining consumption in order to free resources for investment is where it judges that most people would begin to rate marginal consumption above the future benefits flowing from a marginal increase in investment.

This line of argument could of course be criticized in a good many ways. But the fact remains that, if the level of saving is fixed by political decisions about desirable levels of taxation and interest rates, the investment criterion needed is essentially a criterion for allocating investible resources between competing uses rather than a criterion that shows how much should be invested. The usual principle of substitution at the margin would indicate opportunity-cost as the obvious criterion for this purpose. Attempts that have been made to justify the use of a different (usually lower) rate supposed to represent social time preference on the ground that taxes are paid only partly out of income that would have been invested are unconvincing. Those who favour this approach advocate a public sector discount rate which is a hybrid derived by applying the opportunity-cost rate to the portion of marginal tax revenue supposedly withdrawn from private investment, and a (lower) time-preference rate to the rest. Two objections to this procedure (leaving aside the fact that the time-preference rate can only be guessed at) are that resources that have been withdrawn from consumption can in principle be invested anywhere, and need not be restricted to the public sector, and that individuals who are free to save and invest their savings must value £1 of marginal consumption as highly as the present value of the prospective returns from investing £1 in equities, discounted at their own time preference rates.[3] In the view of the author, these objections are decisive. But others have taken the view that, even if the distinction between expenditure that displaces private investment and that which merely displaces consumption is abandoned, there is still a case for using a time preference rate to rank public investments in a merit order, while the balance between public and private investment is held by fixing a minimum ratio greater than 1 which the present value of net receipts/benefits of public investment must bear to the initial cost of the investment. The object is to arrange matters so that a marginal investment in the public sector will confer the same net benefit as a marginal piece of private investment would show if its returns were discounted at the social time preference rate instead of at the (higher) risk rate used by private firms. If the latter is 10%, for example, an investment of 100 by a private firm would be marginal if it yielded an annual return of 16 for ten years. With a social time preference rate of 4% such a stream of returns would have present value 130, so that in this case the ratio of present value of benefits to initial cost that will make the same investment appear marginal in both public and private sectors would be 1·3 : 1. The operative words, however, are 'in this case'. For if we had taken a period of twenty years instead of ten years for comparison the ratio would have been approximately 1·6 : 1, while if we had considered investments with a life of only five years we would have concluded that the ratio ought to be 1·15 : 1. A stipulation that the present value of returns discounted at 4% must be at least 1·3 times capital costs would exclude short-term investments in the public sector offering returns up to 30%, since the present value at 4% of 130 due one year hence is 96·2% of 130, which is obviously less than 1·3 times a first cost of 100. (Obviously it would be possible to 'correct' for these distortions by making special rules for very short- and very long-lived investments in the public sector, but the result of such a process would be that we would have gone a long and complicated way round to arrive at a criterion substantially similar to opportunity-cost.)

The fundamental objection to ranking investments in an order of preference based on present values calculated at a discount rate which is not the opportunity-cost of capital is that, unless we assume that benefits from investment must be consumed as they accrue (i.e. that returns cannot be reinvested), it can be shown that a series of high-yielding short-term investments carried out over a period of time confers more benefit on society than a long-term investment with a lower rate of return spanning the same period.[4] The rate of return on an investment expresses the return per unit of capital outstanding per unit of time, and it will be obvious that, other things equal, an investment with a higher rate of return will confer more benefit than an investment of the same amount carrying a lower rate of return over the same period. Before the choice of an investment with a low rate of return can be justified in preference to one with a higher rate of return that has a lower present value or a lower ratio of present value to capital cost because it is relatively short-lived, it has to be shown that it would not be possible to reinvest the capital released on the termination of the shorter-lived project in such a way that the total benefits over the whole period would not be greater than they will be if the investment with the lower rate of return is chosen. Since in the initial period covered by the life of the less durable investment benefits will be greater (because the rate of return is higher), this condition will be fulfilled only if there is reason to think that opportunities for investment will be more restricted in the relevant future period than in the year in which the choice has to be made, or where 'returns' accrue in non-monetary forms.

In principle, investments excluded by a decision to use limited capital resources for some given purpose are always marginal investments offering returns similar to the marginal productivity of capital. If therefore there are reasons for expecting that the marginal productivity of capital will fall through time, it may not be possible to invest capital becoming available in the future as profitably as capital can now be invested. In these circumstances it may sometimes be rational to prefer an investment whose present value is not quite as high as that of an alternative use of the capital when both are discounted at the current cost of capital, if the second investment has higher present value when both are discounted at the expected future cost of capital, just as when interest rates are higher than they are expected to be on average in the foreseeable future, a long-term bond offering a return above the average rate expected may be a better investment than a short-term bond carrying a slightly higher rate of interest. But this consideration does not support a case for abandoning opportunity-cost in favour of time preference rates of discount. What it does is to illustrate a principle which we noted in connection with the financing plans of private firms (chapter 8) but which we have so far neglected in the context of public investment. The modification required to the rule that the discount rate used in the public sector should measure the opportunity-cost of capital that could in theory be invested in the private sector is simply that account should be taken of any foreseeable changes in the opportunity-cost of capital, by using different discount rates as appropriate to discount costs and receipts falling at different times.

If it is expected that in years 1 to 5 capital available for investment or reinvestment will be able to earn at least 10%, while in years 6 to 10 marginal productivity will be only 6%, the use of a 10% discount rate for the first half of the ten-year period recognizes the fact that £100 received in year 3, for example, is worth the same as £110 received in year 4, while a switch to 6% halfway through the period reflects the fact that, with less profitable opportunities for the employment of capital after year 5, we are indifferent between £100 accruing in year 6 and £106 in year 7. The present value of an investment yielding £1,000 a year for ten years in these conditions would be calculated as follows:

(i)	P.V. in year 0 of 1000 p.a. in years 1–5 at 10% discount	: 3791
(ii) (a)	P.V. in year 5 of 1000 p.a. in years 6–10 at 6% discount	: 4212
(b)	P.V. in year 0 of 4212 in year 5 (10% discount	: 2615
(iii)	P.V. in year 0=(i) plus (ii) (b)	: 6406

Had the cost of capital been expected to remain the same throughout the 10 years, present value in year 0 would have been 6145 if the cost had been 10% throughout or 7360 if the cost of capital had been 6% throughout. Had the cost been expected to rise from 6% to 10% at the end of year 5 (instead of falling from 10% to 6%) the present value of the investment would have been 7053.

We conclude therefore that public investment ought to be appraised by reference to their present values calculated at a discount rate measuring as accurately as possible the opportunity-cost of capital, defined as the return prospectively obtainable on marginal employments of capital in the private sector. Since marginal returns will on conventional assumptions about the shape of demand curves for investible funds vary inversely with the amount of private investment undertaken, this clearly does not provide a criterion for judging how much investment should be undertaken in the public and private sectors combined. But since the amount of capital available for investment depends in practice largely on government decisions about taxation, economists must be concerned primarily with the problem of how best to allocate the investible resources available, the total being taken as a datum. The social time-preference rate, if it can be measured, becomes relevant in certain social benefit calculations where returns do not accrue in the form of monetary receipts to an investing undertaking, and consequently are not directly available for reinvestment. In these cases it will be convenient to calculate terminal values of investments rather than present values. Monetary costs and returns should be cumulated at the opportunity-cost rate, while any non-monetary benefits that can be evaluated should be cumulated at the social time-preference rate if this can be separately identified.[5]

NOTES

[1] *National Income and Expenditure, 1967*, Tables 37, 45, and 78.

[2] M. S. Feldstein: 'Net Social Benefit Calculation and the Public Investment Decision', in *Oxford Economic Papers*, vol. 16, March 1964. See also suggestions for further reading at end of book.

[3] E. J. Mishan: 'Criteria for Public Investment: Some Simplifying Suggestions', *Journal of Political Economy*, vol. 75, April 1967.

[4] J. L. Carr: 'Social Time Preference versus Opportunity Cost in Investment Criteria', *Economic Journal*, vol. LXXVI, December 1966.

[5] E. J. Mishan: 'A Proposed Normalization Procedure for Public Investment Criteria', *Economic Journal*, vol. LXXVII, December 1967.

13

Cost-benefit analysis

In chapter 11 we suggested that there might be a case for subsidizing public transport, and/or for taxing the use of private cars, if it could be shown that a shift from public to private transport by some travellers would impose costs on others (in the shape of delays caused by increased road congestion) that were not fully reflected in the costs falling on those making the shift. This does not mean that the price system works so badly that it should be superseded by some 'higher' criterion for resource allocation. On the contrary, the deficiency is due to the fact that, for various reasons, the price system does not cover the whole field of activity. In the case instanced the man who delays other motorists (and bus passengers) by deciding to take his car to the office instead of catching a bus may with luck get there sooner than he would by bus. He pays for his petrol, and for the extra wear and tear on his car, and he may or may not pay something to park it while he is at work. The total of these costs may or may not add up to more than the bus fare, but even if using his car costs more, the decision whether to go by car or by bus will be taken by the motorist without reference to the costs imposed on others. Even if we assume that roads are paid for out of taxes on petrol and road vehicles—which in form at least they are not—there is no distinction between the tax on a gallon of petrol used in the London rush hour and one used to propel a car along deserted country roads. Yet road space is a scarce resource in London and most other towns at certain times, and as such would command a price if the price system were allowed to work. There have in fact been proposals recently for introducing road-pricing in congested places, and if these are adopted the economic case for subsidizing public transport will be largely if not wholly vitiated. But even if full urban road-pricing one day ensures that road users pay the costs of the congestion they impose, we shall still need a criterion for deciding how much should be invested in improving roads. So good a liberal economist as Adam Smith regarded roads as assets that should be provided by responsible public authorities, and not left to the market to provide. But in the absence of a market test, what criterion have we to help us decide how much should be spent, and how whatever is spent should be allocated?

The price system, working through competitive markets, tends to bring about the production of the kinds and quantities of goods and services that consumers are willing to pay for. When this system does not apply, the connection between investment decisions and demand for final products is broken, and has to be replaced by something else. In the absence of anything better we have to rely on the informed judgment of governments and public bodies, but their decisions cannot be shown to be in any objective sense superior to alternatives. Cost-benefit analysis is essentially designed to enable comparisons to be made between public investments where a market test either does not apply, or works imperfectly because important costs or benefits do not enter into market prices.[1]

Any investment outlay should produce a stream of future benefits, and may involve commitment to certain future costs. In so far as these can be evaluated in monetary terms, discounting can be used to find the present value of the net benefits expected to flow from an investment, and this present value can be compared with the capital cost. If the present value of the net benefits, discounted at a rate that measures the potential productivity in alternative uses of the resources required, exceeds the cost, there is a prima facie case for saying that the investment is socially worth while, and if a number of alternative investments (e.g. different schemes for improving the same road) have to be compared, the one with the highest net present value (present value of benefits less present value of costs) will be the most desirable if all costs and benefits have been correctly valued.

The main difficulty of applying this attractive-sounding method of improving public well-being is that it is seldom easy to identify and quantify all the relevant costs and benefits without either omissions or double-counting, and frequently impossible to convert those that can be identified and quantified into monetary values without arbitrariness. Some benefits or costs may have to be omitted from the calculation because there are no known units in terms of which they can be quantified. Many people dislike the appearance of overhead electricity transmission lines and pylons, but it is impossible to compare one wirescape with another (or with a chicken farm) in terms of so many units of visual disamenity. The best we can do in such a case may be to proceed in some rough-and-ready way such as the following. 'Wirescape A will be seen by 30,000 people every week, and wirescape B by only 20,000. So if the costs are the same, B is less objectionable.' But only, of course, if the annoyance felt by the 30,000 and the 20,000 is comparable. B would certainly not be preferable if it dominated the view from 1000 gardens, while A was seen only briefly through a train window by people who happened to look up from their newspapers. Or we might draw on experience gathered from surveys and questionnaires to estimate the proportion of those to whose view the disfiguring object would be exposed who would object to it so strongly that they would be prepared to pay for its removal, and how much they would be likely to contribute willingly. But all these methods are plainly very unreliable. When the factors that cannot be quantified are relatively unimportant, they can be omitted from the calculation and introduced qualitatively as factors which may influence the decision if the balance between quantifiable costs and benefits is small or uncertain. If two alternative schemes turn out to have very similar net benefits when damage to visual amenity is excluded, the one that does less damage to visual amenity will obviously be preferable —provided everybody is agreed which does less damage. And a project that will obviously damage amenity to some extent turns out to confer only marginal net benefits when amenity is left out of account, it clearly should not be proceeded with. But in many cases a value judgment has to be made, and cost-benefit analysis can only point to the cost, in terms of present value of net benefits foregone, of preserving the amenity. This is of course a valuable function, since it is more meaningful to ask people whether they consider an amenity worth £x to preserve than to ask them whether they are in favour of preserving it without telling them the cost. In the last resort many—perhaps most—economic decisions are influenced by value judgments, and the cynic who knows only the price of everything serves a useful role if his sordid calculations help his non-cynical fellows to decide which of the things they value they will consent to give up in order to have other things they value more. To expect economists to tell people what kind of environment will make them happiest is one degree more futile than expecting them to tell management what risks are worth taking.

Outside the field of the unquantifiable, things are somewhat easier. A great deal of experience, particularly in the U.S.A., has been gained in the application of cost-benefit techniques to the control and development of water resources. Damage done by floods and droughts in the past can be measured, and the statistical probability of recurrence inferred from records. The benefits of irrigation can also be estimated by reference to probable effects on crop values and farming costs, and a price tag can also be put on the commercial value of water supplies to industry. The value of domestic water supplies may be more difficult to quantify, but when the cost of supplying water to households is known it can be compared with household incomes to see whether it is likely to be within most families' means. If there is doubt it is always possible to take a vote, or let those who want water pay for their connections.

Time savings

Time savings crop up frequently in cost-benefit analysis, especially in the field of transport. Most people have some idea of the value of time. There are problems arising from the fact that different people value time quite differently, and the same people may value it more highly on some days than on others. Working time and leisure time are not directly comparable because most people are not in fact able to fix their working hours so that the marginal value to them of an hour's net earnings is the same as the value of another hour's leisure,[2] and there is also the complication that working time is paid for by employers, to whom the cost is the wage gross of tax and plus a profit margin, whereas to the employee the reward for an extra hour's work is the wage less tax at his marginal rate. Thus an hour's overtime for which an employee may receive between 5s. and 10s. after tax could be worth twice as much to his employer. But despite this, if we know approximately how much time will be saved by how many people if some specified transport improvement is made, we can get a fair idea within reasonable limits of its social value.

Transport improvements may also save vehicle operating costs and benefit traders by improving access to formerly inaccessible places. Care has to be taken to avoid double-counting in this last context, since benefits to traders in one locality are likely to be matched by losses to others if change takes the form of diversion of trade from one area to another rather than an increase in real wealth produced. (But if shoppers get better value for their money in the new locality, they at least will benefit, and if lower prices reflect lower real resource costs there is at least the possibility that the resources released will increase national wealth.)

Other transport improvements, particularly road improvements, can be expected to reduce accidents. These have not been easy to evaluate. So far as damage to vehicles is concerned, insurance companies can provide relevant statistics. But death and serious injury are not easily reduced to financial terms, and here we may have to choose between arbitrariness and some form of indirect calculation. We may decide, for example, that it is socially worth while to attempt to reduce the accident rate on all main roads which at present are statistically more dangerous than the national average. Depending on circumstances this might be done by improvements which save time and cost money, or by speed restrictions that cost time and also cost money for enforcement, but are cheaper than the road improvements needed, or by some combination of road improvements and speed restrictions. If the necessary data have been collected experts can form estimates of the costs of the various alternative means of bringing about the results desired, and compare the costs of the relatively modest aim of reducing accident rates on all main roads to the present national average with the more ambitious one of reducing it to the rate prevailing on those lengths of road which are statistically safest.

Opportunity costs and market prices

A third set of problems arises when we have to deal with costs having values in alternative uses that differ from their market prices. A basic difference between cost-benefit and commercial investment analysis is that in the former we deal with opportunity costs all the time, whereas in the latter market prices are the rule unless a firm is considering possible alternative uses for its own human and financial resources. This can make a practical difference to decisions when, for instance, alternative proposals would create a demand for labour (or cause redundancy) in different places. Labour that would almost certainly be employed at much the same wage in some other job if it were not needed for a purpose being considered, obviously has a higher opportunity cost than labour that would be likely to remain unemployed, or be reduced to a much lower standard of earnings, if it was not required for the purpose considered.

There is room for controversy here, for while most kinds of skill are scarce in some places, and some kinds are scarce in most places, time can bring changes which could make nonsense of long-term investment appraisals based on the assumption that the existing pattern of unemployment would endure for years ahead. For one thing, a number of old workers possessing skills that are no longer in demand pass out of the labour force each year and are replaced by a generation of school-leavers who are as yet uncommitted to any particular trade or calling. Most people, especially when they are young, can and will learn new trades and move to new places if the financial incentives are strong enough. There is a danger that, by keeping industries alive to avoid redundancy among workers who have become specialized and unadaptable, we may be drawing a number of young people every year into occupations that employ their talents less efficiently than alternatives which they would enter if the declining industries offered fewer jobs. Moreover if the government is successful in keeping unemployment constant at some acceptable figure, it must be presumed that any increased unemployment among people from a particular industry will in the longer run be offset by reduced unemployment in other industries, since if this did not happen there would be a ratchet effect and unemployment would increase continuously through time. If this does not happen we may reasonably assume that redundancies that have taken place have not permanently affected the level of employment in the country.

These thoughts, however, should not blind us to the fact that much of the re-absorption and re-allocation of labour necessary to prevent overall unemployment rising comes about only because conscious efforts are being made all the time to steer jobs towards places where unemployment exists. It is certainly and obviously true that the cost of labour employed in factories where jobs are hard to find is in a meaningful sense less than the cost of similar labour employed in London, and even if the pattern of unemployment is expected to change over a number of years, application of discounting techniques will still weight opportunity costs in the present and the immediate future more heavily than costs in later years. We are likely to go wrong as a result of taking current opportunity costs into account only if we assume without justification that these costs will remain unaltered for years ahead. Thus if we are considering where to locate an installation, and one possible site is in an area where there is virtually no unemployment and all the labour needed would have to be withdrawn from other jobs where its estimated average value (marginal product) is £1000 per man-year, while an alternative site is located where there is so much unemployment that the whole labour force could be recruited from the unemployed, it will be right, other things equal, to cost a labour force of 100 men at £100,000 in one location and zero in the other during the first year. But if the government has plans for reducing disparities between unemployment levels in different areas it would be wrong to carry this cost difference through the life of the investment. Suppose our best guess is that unemployment in the second area will be reduced over five years to a level at which it would be reasonable to assume that two prospective employees out of every three would find work within that time, while the average pressure of demand for labour in the first area can be expected to be slightly less intense in the future so that, again on average, one man in every ten prospective employees would be out of work if the project did not go ahead in that area. The labour cost components of the respective cash flows would be, in terms of opportunity costs, as follows, calling the site in the area of low unemployment A and the alternative site B.

Year:	0	1	2	3	4	
Site A	−1000	−900	−900	−900	−900	
Site B	0	−133	−266	−400	−533	
Year	5	6	7	8	9	10
Site A	−900	−900	−900	−900	−900	−900
Site B	−666	−666	−666	−666	−666	−666

By discounting these two streams the present value of prospective labour opportunity costs can be found for each location, and differences compared with differences in other costs and benefits to establish which site is on balance preferable in the light of conditions expected to prevail during the life of the installation.

Consistency in decision-making

It is sometimes suggested that all public investments should be appraised by taking all quantifiable costs and benefits into account. It seems reasonable enough in principle to say that, since society as a whole is the only counterpart of the shareholders in private firms, social benefits and costs should be taken fully into account when public investment plans are drawn up. There are, however, two difficulties which at least deserve recognition, one practical and the other theoretical. The practical difficulty is that cost-benefit analysis generally requires considerably more expertise than does the appraisal of investment in commercial terms, and leaves scope for differences of opinion as to the monetary valuations to be placed on many costs and benefits which have no market price tags, as well as some intangibles which may be difficult to quantify even without valuing. If planners in different industries, or different divisions of the same industry, differ in their subjective estimation of these factors, consistency in decision-making will not easily be achieved. On the other hand one's mind boggles at the prospect of putting all public investment proposals, or even all major schemes, before a central evaluation board which would be a sort of super holding company controlling the deployment of capital throughout the public sector; even companies of quite modest size have learned that over-centralization of decision-making can reduce efficiency, and in communist countries the absurdities that result from detailed central planning are a stock-in-trade of comedians. In the author's opinion it is at least equally difficult to imagine that a comprehensive set of rules for cost-benefit analysis could be produced and circulated to managements in the public sector, with periodic amendments notified and pasted in like amendments to the Manual of Military Law or an office telephone directory. If there is one thing that early experience of cost-benefit analysis has taught its practitioners, it is that it cannot be done by the book. The only way to go about a problem is to look at it from all angles, see what elements can be identified, try to quantify those that can be identified as relevant, and then try to find some non-arbitrary way of putting money values on the resulting numbers. We may one day make cost-benefit analysis into a science, but at present it is very much an art, for the practice of which imagination, flair, and a streak of heroism are generally required. Some guiding principles can be established, but their application in particular cases usually requires the exercise of both judgment and imagination.

The theoretical reason for expressing reservations about the desirability of basing all public investment decisions on cost-benefit analysis instead of financial profitability is that, even if the discount rate correctly represented the opportunity cost of capital invested in the private sector, a case could be made out for arguing that the result would be over-investment in the public sector. This is not because cost-benefit analysis goes wider than financial appraisal. There is no reason to think that externalities are more important on the benefits side than on the costs side. The root of the trouble is that cost-benefit analysis generally includes the consumers' surplus, which is by definition excluded from financial appraisals.

If we consider the case for electrifying a railway line as it would appear to a management concerned to answer the question whether such a course would be financially profitable, the solution is found by estimating the likely effects on future cash flow of lower train operating and maintenance costs together with higher receipts from passengers if an improved quality of service increases the numbers who travel at any given level of fares. The present value of these future cash benefits, plus any additional items such as reduced costs of replacing locomotives, is compared with the initial cost, and if the present value of the future cash benefits discounted at the appropriate (opportunity-cost) rate is less than the initial cost, the investment will appear financially worth while.

If cost-benefit analysis is applied to this project, the cost savings made by the railway will need modification only if the prices paid for resources such as labour diverge from their potential value in alternative uses (opportunity costs), or if there are external economies, such as cleaner air, or diseconomies, such as overhead transmission lines. Unless a significant number of railwaymen are likely to remain permanently unemployed as a result of staff economies made possible by electrification, the opportunity costs are unlikely to differ greatly from the market prices of resources saved, and if there is some divergence there is no presumption that it will go one way rather than the other. If factor markets work perfectly, market prices will equal transfer values; if markets are imperfect the transfer values may be higher or lower than prices paid by the railway. But on the benefits side there is a presumption that the value of benefits will exceed the additional cash receipts, which were all that entered into the calculation of financial profitability.

Suppose the line in question is 80 miles long, and that after electrification 1000 more people travel over its whole length in each direction every week. If the fare paid by each is £1 the increase in receipts will be £2000 per week. Suppose that the fare of £1 is 10s. more than the fare by an alternative road service from which the extra rail passengers are diverted, the reason for their altered choice being that the new rail service takes an hour less than the road journey, whereas the old rail service took only half an hour less than the road service. Before electrification, the railway carried those passengers who valued time savings at £1 per hour or more (since they paid 10s. extra fare to save half an hour on the journey), plus those who paid the extra fare because it was less than the value they placed on intangible factors such as comfort and safety. Assuming that the electric service is neither safer nor more comfortable than the old service, the passengers who divert to rail after electrification will be those who value time savings at between 10s. and 20s. per hour, since those who value the hour now saved if they go by train at £1 or more used the pre-electric train service, while those who value an hour at less than 10s. will still prefer road. If we assume that the average passenger diverted to rail values the hour saved as 15s., the value of the time saved on the extra 2000 journeys made each week will be £1500. Also saved are the resources formerly used to transport these people by road. If the road fare of 10s. just covered average costs the saving will be £1000 per week. So we have benefits of £2500 a week (compared with additional receipts of £2000) before considering what may be the largest benefit item of all, namely the value of time saved by those who travelled by rail before electrification. Even on this rather conservative assumption (looked at this way round) that electrification brings a 50% increase in passenger traffic, and that half those who travelled formerly did so on account of comfort and safety and place no value on time savings at all, electrification will save half an hour on each 2000 journeys made each week by people who value their time at 20s. an hour or more, so that if we make the still more conservative assumption that none of them values time at more than £1 an hour (i.e. they all value it at £1 an hour) the minimum value of these savings is £1000 per week, giving a total benefit of £3500 compared with the additional cash receipts of £2000.

There is no satisfactory way of correcting for the fact that cost-benefit analysis normally takes account of consumers' surplus. (Since an increase in consumers' surplus is in itself a desirable thing, we ought perhaps to put this the other way round and say there is no satisfactory way of correcting for the fact that investment appraisal in terms of financial profitability neglects consumers' surplus.) Using a higher discount rate in cost-benefit analysis is not the answer, because this would distort choices between short- and long-term benefits without reference to consumers' surplus. Nor can we brush the problem aside on the grounds that many investments, notably those directed purely to saving costs, generate no consumers' surplus. If these are acceptable uses of capital when they show returns of 8%, the argument runs, why should we not accept investments which cost-benefit shows to yield 8%, including consumers' surplus, even if the latter would not yield 8% in hard cash? The trouble with this line of reasoning is that to use in the public sector an investment criterion which was less stringent than the criterion used in the private sector (because the former admitted consumers' surplus while the latter did not) would bias the allocation of scarce capital towards the public sector, where we would be undertaking a number of projects which would not be acceptable in the private sector. (These would be investments which yielded 8% or more in cost-benefit terms, but less than 8% financial return.) The point of appraising public investment by using a discount rate equal to the opportunity cost of capital invested in the private sector would largely be lost.

We have suggested that the universal employment of cost-benefit techniques to appraise public investment would militate against consistency in decision-making in a mixed economy, whatever theoretical advantages it might have in a centrally planned economy. How, then, should these techniques be used? Their usefulness in many cases is beyond doubt, since the attempt to quantify and evaluate all the gains and losses likely to result from a major public investment decision can be a useful exercise in itself. Even if it does not point clearly to one solution to a problem, it makes it less likely that decisions will be unduly influenced by factors which turn out on examination to be less significant than others which may have attracted less attention. It is no denigration of cost-benefit analysis to state its limitations.

Perhaps the right view to take at the present time is that, in a mixed economy where decisions are necessarily taken on grounds of financial profitability in the private sector, resource allocation is unlikely to suffer much damage if similar criteria are applied by trading bodies in the public sector, provided that cost-benefit techniques can be and are employed where social costs or benefits, or externalities that do not affect the cash flows of investing bodies, seem likely to be important, so that reliance on market criteria could not be trusted to give the right answers. (Obvious examples can be found in the field of urban public transport, but the usefulness of cost-benefit is by no means restricted to this field.) When investment decisions have to be taken by public concerns that are not trading bodies there is usually no market test available, so that cost-benefit analysis is the only alternative to inspired guesswork. The qualifications about comparability of financial and social net benefits or rates of return, which arise chiefly because of the exclusion of consumers' surplus from the former, should be allowed for in some fashion wherever possible; we should not wish to take out consumers' surplus from individual calculations, because an increase in surplus is a genuine social benefit not to be despised. But if we are aiming to allocate a limited quantity of investible resources as productively as possible in a mixed economy, we shall do well to look rather suspiciously at investments 'justified' by cost-benefit calculations which show discounted benefits exceeding discounted costs by rather slender margins. There may well be opportunities for employing capital more productively in projects which are financially profitable, and also add to consumers' surplus.

NOTES

[1] A. R. Prest and R. Turvey: 'Cost Benefit Analysis: A Survey', *Economic Journal*, vol. LXXV, December 1965.

[2] People who would rather work shorter hours will value leisure at the margin higher than working time, and vice versa.